Land-Grant College

Review

Issue No. Four

Land-Grant College

Review

Cover and title page artwork created specifically for the
Land-Grant College Review by Steve Keene.
Gallery Information: SKSK, 85 Wythe Avenue, Williamsburg, Brooklyn
info@stevekeene.com/www.stevekeene.com

Distributed by:

Bernhard DeBoer
113 East Center Street
Nutley, NJ 07110
tel. 973 667 9300

Ingram Periodicals
18 Ingram Boulevard
La Vergne, TN 37086
tel. 800 627 6247

Single copies: $14 plus $3 for postage and handling. Subscription
rate (two issues): $20 plus $4 for postage and handling. Canadian
and foreign subscribers add $7 per issue surface mail and remit in
U.S. funds. Make checks payable to Land-Grant College Review.

Land-Grant College Review, Inc., a not-for-profit corporation, is
fiscally sponsored by the New York Foundation for the Arts,
a 501 (c)(3) organization. Donations are tax deductible to the fullest
extent of the law.

International Standard Book Number: 0-9728678-3-X
International Standard Serial Number: 1549-0061

Land-Grant College Review, P.O. Box 1164, New York 10159-1164
Land-Grant College Review, Inc., New York City
editors@lgcr.org/www.lgcr.org

Edited *by* DAVE KOCH & JOSH MELROD

Executive Editor:	DAVID SCHUMAN
Artistic Director:	TUCKER CAPPARELL
Design:	AHL & CO./PETER J. AHLBERG
Editor-At-Large:	TARA WRAY
Director of Development:	RYAN MILLER
Editorial Assistants:	ELIZABETH HARTSIG
	SHENA MCAULIFFE
Reader:	DANIEL O'MALLEY
Intern:	KELLY BRIDGES

Contents

LOVE BITES

BY

NICHOLAS MONTEMARAND

LOVE BITES:
AN OFFICIAL REPORT

by Nicholas Montemarano

1.1

See a group of children in Uganda gather around a man they call Kony or Selindi or Ali Salango or Jim Rickey or Who Are You, depending on what spirit he says is speaking through him. The man asks the children who is here, who is here, who is speaking to you, and one child says Selindi because Selindi is a woman who speaks quietly and only to give directions, when to cook, when to wash, when to be silent. The man asks again who is here, who is speaking, and one child says Jim Rickey because Jim Rickey is a dead American soldier who is mostly sad. Again, who is speaking, and the children say Ali Salango, they say Kony, they say Selindi again, Jim Rickey again. No, no, no, who is speaking to you! Not one of the children will say the name, so he will say it for them: Who Are You is speaking and he has a job for you. If you do not complete this job, Who Are You will kill you and drink your blood.

   —It was because the girl tried to escape. She was my age, fourteen, and her name was Adok, and I know this because she helped them abduct me five months earlier. Kony gave her to his commanders to be their wife. My job was to cook and gather firewood. No, I did not have hard feelings for her because she helped them abduct me. You did what you were told to do. When Who Are You told us to bite that girl to death we did what we were told. There were ten of us. My first thought was how do you bite someone to death. I had never bitten someone. My fear was not just that it would hurt her but that it would hurt me too. What does it feel like to bite into someone, all the way through like that? I cannot answer that question because I did not bite all the way through. At first no one did—they must have had the same fear, or must not have known how. But Who Are You had his commanders point their guns at us. He said we must bite to kill or we would be killed. The others started to bite all the way through. You would think this cannot be done, but it can. You would think the flesh is too thick for human teeth. I was right there with them, up close, and that is how I saw. But I did not bite all the way through. I did not draw blood. I did put my mouth on her, I did bite, but only enough to give the impression that I was killing her. I did not kill her like the others did. But I was up close, so I saw how they turned themselves into animals, making grunting sounds like pigs or wild dogs. The whole time the girl was pleading with Kony to spare her life, saying that she would never try to escape again, but Kony was not Kony, he was Who Are You. She was bleeding from her face, from her ears, from her lips, from everywhere, but she did not die. Then we were told to pinch her, so we pinched. This did not draw blood, and I am not sure why we were told to do this. I did this because it did not draw blood and that meant I was not killing her. Then we were told to get in a line. The first in line was given a log and was made to beat the girl about her face. After a while the next in line was given the log. Then the next. The boys hit harder than the girls, and the boy two in front of me killed her. He was big for his age and grunted like an animal. I could see that the girl was dead, that her spirit had left her body. I have seen other dead children and that is how I knew. The moment the spirit leaves, you know. The body becomes a corpse and you can see this. So by the time I was given the log to beat her, I was not beating her, I was not killing her. All this happened two months ago in the Gulu district. Then they let some of us go for amnesty. I came here to the Palabek Kal refugee camp because I am a refugee and do not know where my family is. Some people say that if you smear yourself with shea nut butter you cannot be killed. But I cannot find any shea nut butter.

2.1

—We got the dog because we weren't one hundred percent sure we wanted a child.

—No, certainly not. We did not treat our dog like a child. Not like some dog owners treat their dogs like children. No, we would not say that.

—I believe my husband was more attached to the dog.

—My wife was very attached to the dog. She was the one who trained the dog while I was at work.

—The dog would greet my husband when he came home

with a ball or anything she could fit into her mouth and her tail would knock over glasses and lamps and she would make the cutest whimpering noise.

—We might have treated the dog more like a child than we ever thought we would, but certainly not as much as some people. We never spent two hundred dollars on fur booties so that during winter our dog wouldn't burn her paws on rock salt. Forty dollars, but never two hundred.

—We never thought something like this would ever happen.

—Sure, we considered the dog family if by family you mean did we bring her to family gatherings and buy her presents on Christmas and on her birthday. What we did for the dog we did because, facts are facts, our dog was simply the best dog anyone could ever have. The sweetest disposition—always wanted to please, was good with kids and other dogs.

—A complete shock. We never saw it coming, and when you don't see something coming....

—Not like some we've seen at the dog park. You know the kinds of dogs their owners have to keep a short leash because God knows what they'll do. We're not being judgmental—some dogs have been abused and who can blame them for being the way they are. We're just saying we were lucky to have the dog we had.

—Devastating, obviously.

—She had two red rubber bones, one pink rubber bone, two indestructible rubber balls that looked like tennis balls.

—What was even more devastating was we'd just finished reassuring the mother that yes our dog was friendly.

—Whenever we gave her a real tennis ball, forget it. She went wild for the smell of them, then she'd tear them apart. But most dogs do this—it doesn't mean they're violent.

—I can't even count how many times. Dozens and dozens— all the time mothers would ask if their kids could pet our dog. She was part German shepherd, which is maybe why they asked.

—A few stuffed animals—one of them was a stuffed monkey. If we gave her anything stuffed, forget it.

—At first the boy was petting her and the dog was just sitting there. Then she turned to lick the boy's face and we were all like oh how cute, look how she's giving you kisses, that means she loves you, and all that cutesy stuff you say to kids.

—Usually dry food, but sometimes a burger or a hot dog or a few slices of roast beef. And we had dog biscuits, which she liked, and these peanut butter flavored things she would gobble up—my God, she would have eaten the whole bag if we'd given it to her. And Greenies—she liked those. They're good for the teeth, which is why they're shaped like little toothbrushes. But never from the table. She wasn't a beggar. We were very lucky, I'm telling you.

—But then the mother started yelling look out, look out, oh my God, someone help!

—Our favorite pet name for her was Fuzzy Galoot, though we also called her Baby Big Ears because when she was a puppy she had these hugs ears.

—We have no idea why.

—That we had to put her down was—well, it was just about the worst thing. We were both with her. She was scared, but no more scared than she was of thunder. During thunderstorms was the only time we let her in bed. Otherwise, no way. But when we put her down, she knew. Dogs knows things—they're not stupid.

—To have this happen was like having a normal child, a perfectly well-adjusted and well-behaved child, and then suddenly, in one moment, that child turns violent.

—Newman.

—The boy's okay except some scarring on his face the doctor says will fade.

—No reason except we liked the name.

—We had no choice, really. If your dog does something like that, I mean, how can you ever trust that animal again, especially if you're thinking about kids.

—I was against putting her down. I would not have done it. But my wife wants to have children. We both do.

—We will never have another dog.

—I'd like to get another dog.

3.1

—I don't understand why everyone can't seem to understand. For God's sake, the girl came at him with paint on her fingers. I'll be the first to admit that my son wasn't the best behaved, but to say what they're saying about him. I'm his father, okay, so maybe I'm not the most objective, maybe I feel their fingers pointed at me. Not maybe. But when you're five years old and another kid comes at your face with paint as if to put it in your eyes—that's what he thought she was going to do—what's so criminal about defending yourself? People are using the word criminal, which is just—which is outrageous. And the way that teacher is describing what happened—she's had it out for Leo since day one. To say that our son was quote possessed and that she could quote see demons in his eyes and that quote it wasn't like it was a boy doing what he was doing but more like a beast. Of course she's going to say something like that when (a) she's ultra-religious and even spent a few years in a convent, and (b) the girl with paint on her fingers is her sister's granddaughter. What kind of testimony do you think she's going to give? She keeps talking about all the blood and how the other children were traumatized, but what about my son's blood? Let's not forget that he was the first to bleed, and we all know that at the sight of your own blood you can sometimes get upset or angry and maybe want to defend yourself. They don't like to emphasize that when the girl came at my son with paint on her fingers my son's first reaction wasn't to attack her but was to turn around and run away. That's how dangerous he is—he runs away from paint. When he turned to run, he hit his head on the corner of a desk and that's why he has five stitches. No one likes to talk about my son's five stitches. All everyone talks about is the—Listen, I feel badly for the girl and her family. I want to go on record as saying that. If I had a daughter and she ever came home having been bitten by a boy in her class, you better believe I'd be up there looking for answers. So I don't blame her parents for looking for answers. But please, for God's sake, listen to every side of the story. Don't just listen to a half-nun who's your blood relative. Don't just listen to kids who've had it out for my son since the day he walked into that school. First thing they did the first day—I saw it—was make fun of Leo's sneakers because they were white sneakers he'd colored in black with a magic marker. My wife and I told him that he might want to wear a new pair of sneakers, but those were the sneakers he wanted, and any good parenting book will tell you that in a case like that, so what if the kid wants to wear white sneakers he's colored in black. As long as it's not hurting anyone, so what. So from day one the other kids labeled ours as different. He didn't have any close friends, admitted, but whose fault is that? And now to bring in a psychiatrist for all the children to make sure they're okay about what happened— I think that's a bit too much. Not to mention the quote special meeting for all concerned parents, which they tried to keep from us. Not only did we find out about it, but we had one of our friends report back to us about what was said. One of the fathers brought a book on criminology and tried to label our son as some kind of Charles Manson in training, which we think is borderline slanderous. To say there are fourteen characteristics of a serial killer and my kid has nine and Jeffrey Dahmer had only seven? If I had been there, I swear to God. Our son has a few problems, but no more than most kids have.

Believe me, we're not happy that our son bit that girl. We don't take this lightly. Not at all. In fact, we've already disciplined him. No video games or TV for two months. That will hit him where it hurts, trust me. We'd be more than willing to have him write a letter of apology to the girl if she'd only write a letter of apology for coming at our son with paint and giving him five stitches.

4.1

Alleged victim claims she did not know who alleged assailant was when alleged assailant first approached her in club and offered to buy her a drink. Alleged victim further claims she accepted drink from alleged assailant and engaged in what she describes as polite conversation until drink was finished and alleged assailant offered alleged victim second drink, which she admits was technically her third drink as she had one before alleged assailant approached her. Alleged victim admits that upon finishing third drink (second bought by alleged assailant) she began to recognize alleged assailant's face but was not sure from where. Alleged victim claims that only when she was almost finished with her drink (alleged victim also claims that alleged assailant urged her to drink her drink quickly so he could buy her another) did she begin to understand that alleged assailant was famous, that she knew his face from either television or movies. Alleged victim claims that even at this point, after three drinks, after realizing man buying drinks was celebrity, she engaged in what she continues to describe as polite conversation about drinks, clubbing (alleged victim admits she told alleged assailant she was a regular at club but now claims she said this to impress him, not, she further claims, to seduce him), where she lives, where alleged assailant lives, clothes they were wearing (alleged victim was wearing black thigh-length skirt, black boots, cropped sleeveless shirt that read ITALIANS ARE EASY which she claims she was wearing ironically and offers as proof of irony that she is not Italian but half-German, half-Irish; alleged assailant was wearing jeans, black button−down shirt untucked and unbuttoned, white t-shirt with Superman crest in front center, black blazer, white sneakers). Alleged victim claims she did not know alleged assailant's identity until friend of alleged assailant walked past and winked at alleged assailant and said, Hey, Big Kahuna, which alleged victim recognized as name of character from her favorite teen movie from years ago. Alleged victim claims that upon hearing name and attaching name to face of alleged assailant she knew who he was and wanted to ask him why he had made only a few movies since his most famous movie yet somehow managed to remain in celebrity spotlight especially in tabloids which alleged victim has confessed to reading occasionally if cover story involves celebrities she admires or is intrigued by. Alleged victim claims alleged assailant is not celebrity she particularly admires or has been intrigued by and describes alleged assailant as quote a star who was off my radar pretty much. Alleged victim claims polite conversation continued until polite conversation exhausted itself, whereupon alleged assailant offered again to buy alleged victim third (really her fourth) drink. Alleged victim claims she politely refused drink but alleged assailant persisted and that she refused again but that alleged assailant persisted and that to change subject alleged victim told alleged assailant that he looked familiar and that alleged assailant said, Maybe you know me from your dreams, which alleged victim claims she remembers word-for-word because she could not wait to tell her roommate, who was out of town, when she got back into town, about such a quote tired pick-up line from a former teen movie star almost twice her age. Alleged victim claims she did not find alleged assailant attractive but neither did she find him unattractive, which in retrospect she claims had more to do with alleged assailant's having been in numerous teen movies including what she might consider her favorite, even though alleged assailant did not play lead but rather important supporting role as wealthy school bully on wrestling team who got any girl he wanted, and maybe that had a lot to do, or so alleged victim claims, with her decision to accept alleged assailant's invitation to go back to his place where they could have another drink (her fourth) and where he could show her why he looked so familiar. Alleged victim claims she and alleged assailant left club together alone and walked approximately twenty minutes to alleged assailant's alleged apartment. Alleged victim claims doorman opened door for her and alleged assailant and gave alleged assailant a look alleged victim claims was a sort of wink without winking, which alleged victim took to mean alleged assailant brings back many different women to his apartment. Alleged victim claims this did not deter her from going up to alleged assailant's apartment because in a strange way alleged assailant's tired pick-up line and doorman's wink without winking made her feel like she was hanging out with a character from her favorite teen movie. Alleged victim claims that inside apartment alleged assailant mixed alleged victim very strong drink that tasted like gin with a splash of juice and that she nursed drink. Alleged victim claims alleged assailant put DVD in DVD player and sat as close to her as possible without touching her on couch. Alleged victim claims she and alleged assailant engaged in polite conversation but that she could tell by alleged assailant looking from her eyes to her lips that he wanted to kiss her. Alleged victim claims she looked away from alleged assailant often enough to prevent him from trying to kiss her but that she was not adverse to the idea of kissing alleged assailant but wanted to kiss him on her own terms. Alleged victim claims that when polite conversation exhausted itself alleged assailant put arm around alleged victim and pressed play on DVD player remote control, starting alleged victim's favorite teen movie, which she could have predicted was DVD alleged assailant had put into DVD player. Alleged victim claims she gave alleged assailant confused look as if she did not know why alleged assailant had put in this particular teen movie. Alleged victim claims she did not want to hurt alleged assailant's feelings by letting him know she knew who he was and thereby taking away his chance to surprise her. Alleged victim claims alleged assailant appears in first scene as high school wrestler wearing high school wrestling uniform (this has been confirmed) and that alleged victim looked from screen to alleged assailant, back to screen, back to alleged assailant, then pretended to recognize him even though movie was made almost twenty years ago when alleged assailant was twenty and alleged victim was six. Alleged victim claims that at this point she asked alleged assailant if he was actor on screen wearing high school wrestling uniform and alleged assailant did not say yes but smiled as if to say yes. Alleged victim claims she and alleged assailant watched approximately thirty minutes of teen movie (alleged assailant continually asking alleged victim if he could freshen her drink, alleged victim politely declining while imagining telling roommate about all this when roommate got back into town) until kissing scene in which alleged assailant's character kisses girl who is not girlfriend. Alleged victim claims she playfully slapped alleged assailant's thigh and said, You bad boy, upon which alleged assailant began kissing alleged victim's neck and ears much as alleged assailant's movie character was kissing girl who was not girlfriend's neck and ears. Alleged victim says she did not stop alleged assailant because such a pick-up move— taking cues from a fictional character he played in a teen movie almost twenty years ago—was quote so shockingly lame that it nearly paralyzed her. Alleged victim claims she was also thinking about what she would be able to tell her roommate when her roommate got back into town. Alleged victim claims she did not feel that she was in danger at that point and that alleged assailant's kisses during movie were like getting a massage and that she wanted to make him wait a while before turning to kiss him back. Alleged victim claims alleged assailant started gently nibbling on her neck but that nibbles progressed into what she describes as bites. Alleged victim claims that only when bites became painful and she tried to turn her head away from alleged assailant did she realize that alleged assailant's teeth were fully clamped onto her neck. Alleged victim claims that even when she started screaming, even when she punched alleged assailant's chest, even when she threw remote control at television, even when she told him, Get the fuck off me you fucking freak, alleged assailant would not release grip on alleged victim's neck. Alleged victim claims that it wasn't until she left building that she realized how much she was bleeding and that she needed medical attention. Alleged victim claims she did not remember, until reminded by her roommate when her roommate got back into town, that alleged assailant also had important but not starring role in teen vampire movie fifteen years ago. Alleged victim claims that this connection, when it was pointed out to her, quote creeped her out.

4.2

Both alleged victim and alleged assailant remain alleged because alleged victim dropped charges before a trial date was set. Alleged victim's lawyers were convinced, and convinced her, that she could win, that she could get millions, that the defendant—because he was married at the time of the alleged offense (his wife and two children were in their home in Los Angeles)—might very likely want to settle. But alleged assailant did not want to settle. Alleged assailant alleged that alleged victim, having seen his vampire movie and having been a big fan of his since she was a girl, asked him to bite her neck, and that he was reluctant at first because (a) he was married and loved his wife and children, and (b) he knew how sometimes fans liked to sue celebrities just to make easy money, and that the public often liked to see celebrities taken down, and that he could see a disaster brewing. Alleged assailant alleged that he explained all this to alleged victim, who said quote, I'm not one of those crazy people who would ever do something like that. I went to college. I have a good job. End quote. Only after some more deliberation and discussion, alleged assailant alleged, did he begin to nibble alleged victim's neck, upon which alleged victim allegedly asked alleged assailant to bite harder, upon which he asked her if she was sure, upon which she said yes. Alleged assailant further alleged that he was not alleged assailant but rather victim in what he referred to as a lawsuit trap. Alleged assailant also referred to alleged victim as unstable marriage wrecker, and then he clarified this by saying that he did not mean that alleged victim was wrecker of unstable marriage but that alleged victim was unstable and that he wanted to see his quote quoted correctly and fully in the papers the next day or he would sue. If anyone should be sued, alleged assailant said, it should be the press or alleged victim for wrecking his marriage and ruining his kids' lives. What did he do, alleged assailant wanted to know, except honor a longtime fan's request. Alleged assailant admitted poor judgment but admitted no further fault. Alleged victim remained steadfast for four months, but two weeks before a trial date was set she dropped her suit against alleged assailant. Oddly, alleged assailant seemed almost disappointed, claiming he would have liked an opportunity to show the world just how much of a liar alleged victim was. Alleged victim cited stress and harassment as the two most important factors in her decision. Stress from having every aspect of her personal life scrutinized, including her sexual history, which included two abortions (alleged victim claimed that the only reason this information came out was because the girlfriend of one of the men who had impregnated her was still bitter) and a previous rape charge that she eventually dropped (alleged victim claimed that alleged rapist leaked this information), and her psychological history, including how many years she had spent in therapy (seven, off and on) and what prescriptions she had filled over the years (Xanax, Ativan, Zoloft, most recently Paxil). Harassment, alleged victim claimed, came mostly from men, but sometimes from women, all of whom would make jokes about biting or vampires or about her sexual and psychological history that had been leaked to the tabloids. It is not the business of this committee to side with one side or the other or to declare who suffered more, but rather to state the facts. One year after dropping charges alleged victim's boyfriend nibbled on alleged victim's neck, whereupon alleged victim hit boyfriend's face with the back of her hand, breaking his nose. Alleged assailant's career, as many people know, has been resurrected. Movie producers cite alleged assailant's quote newfound sexiness in the face of the charges he faced. They further cite that a poll of women eighteen to forty showed that alleged assailant was among the celebrities women in that age demographic were most likely to want to have sex with. In the two years since charges were dropped alleged assailant has made four films, the most recent of which was the buzz at Sundance, even though it did not win any of the juried prizes. Some movie critics are saying alleged assailant's performance is Oscar-worthy. Alleged victim alleges she has not seen this film nor any of alleged assailant's new films, nor will she ever, nor will she ever again watch any of alleged assailant's films she used to admire. However, alleged victim's ex-boyfriend— alleged victim of alleged victim's blow to face—alleges that he and new girlfriend ran into alleged victim at New York opening of alleged assailant's most recent film. This has not been confirmed and so must remain, as must much of this report, an allegation. Other than what we have reported here, nothing further is alleged at this time.

3.2

—We take the one seat together, the three of us, three times daily, so I guess you can say we take the three seat. Once in the morning, before Leo leaves for school, once before dinner, and once before bed. Fifteen minutes each for a total of forty-five, which is considered a good amount. We don't preoccupy ourselves with the past. What's done is done. We focus on each breath—that's all there is. Now we say the word now a lot. Now I tie my tie; now I wash my face; now I bite a bite of cake. There are close-minded people out there who believe that meditation is weird, that you become a kind of zombie, or that it's only for people in cults. But we're proof that that's not true because we're not zombies and we're not in a cult. We're just human beings trying to witness what every present moment gives us. To live in harmony with the world is what we want. I read about meditation as a way to reverse violent inclinations in your child in the book Dr. Stevens gave us when we were on his show about violent children a few months ago. One reason I wrote to Dr. Stevens is what happened at school. The biting incident. My husband doesn't like to call it the biting incident, he calls it the five stitches incident, referring to the five stitches Leo had to have, but one thing I'm learning is to see things for what they really are, and it is true to say that what happened at school was the biting incident. There is no shame in saying that; there is only shame in not saying what is, or in saying what is not. And even then, there need not be shame. What's important is to know why you're saying what you're saying, why you're thinking what you're thinking, why you're denying what is for what is not. The other reason I wrote to Dr. Stevens is that the biting incident was the culmination of years of unhealthy behavior on the part of our son. Leo had a violent temper even at home, especially when we disciplined him or asked him if he had done something he wasn't supposed to do. He banged his head on the wall when we didn't give him what he wanted. Several times he smeared his own feces on the bathroom wall. He liked to pull off the legs of bugs and frogs, which my husband said was our son just being a boy. But that's not what Dr. Stevens said. Being on the show was a turning point for us as a family because Dr. Stevens looked us straight in our eyes and told us we were in a very serious, borderline dangerous, situation. That was when I cried on the show and told Dr. Stevens and my husband and even our son, who was up on stage with us, that I feared for my own life and for the lives of the children in our neighborhood. Just even saying that was a relief. Dr. Stevens is not known for his outward sympathy, so he did not hug me or even tell me everything was going to be okay. He's more of a tough love doctor. He has a mustache and a shaved head and a southern accent, in case you've never seen the show. I expected him to tell us that it was all genes, but he started asking my husband questions and referring to statements my husband had made on the questionnaire we filled out before the show. He even played some video footage of my husband interacting with Leo, which showed my husband letting Leo get away with things and disregarding his violent behavior as boys will be boys. The exact turning point was when Dr. Stevens looked at my husband and said, Do you not understand that this boy is starved for male attention? I mean, what do you not understand about that? Just hearing the almost harsh tone of his voice towards my husband made me cry again, but this time in a good way, because now I knew I had someone on my side. In addition to telling us how to discipline Leo, such as one strike and no TV, two strikes and no video games, three strikes and everything comes out of his room but the bed, all of which we implemented, Dr. Stevens also gave us a book on meditation, focusing specifically on family meditation, which you would think goes against the whole notion of meditation, being that it's a private thing, but the three of us take the one seat together, and it works out fine that way. Or at least sometimes it does. Even when things don't work out, that's okay because things never don't work out. That's something I learned from the meditation book, which isn't a book on being a Buddhist, lots of Catholics and Protestants and other Christians meditate too. To say that everything that ever happens is okay isn't amoral, it just means that everything that happens is in harmony with the *Tao* (which is Chinese for *Way* or *Path*) and that the *Tao* is wherever you find yourself. So our *Tao* included Leo biting a girl at school and us going on Dr. Stevens's show and now us meditating, though my husband has been making excuses lately and therefore so has Leo, and sure enough last week Leo clogged a toilet at school with wads of toilet paper and flushed and flushed. Until the toilet incident, we were on the right path, I think. (No, I must remember that everything is the right path, even Leo clogging toilets.) We even have silent days where no one is allowed to speak, and the teachers at Leo's new school—we changed schools after the biting incident, not to run away from anything, but to enter a new present—are part of this plan, and they know not to call on Leo even if he raises his hand. We also have patience days, where our entire focus is on waiting for things. If Leo asks me to pass the butter, I'll wait sometimes fifteen minutes before passing him the butter, and even if he cries or throws his plate on the floor, I will not pass him the butter until he's learned patience. The teachers help with this, too. They know which days are Leo's patience days, and they wait extra long to answer his questions. I'm not trying to say that just from taking the one seat Leo is a saint, but he's more mindful. That's the whole purpose of taking the one seat—not necessarily to be a better person, whatever better means, but to be more awake. Some people think meditation is almost like sleeping, but it's not. You're hyper-aware, but only of the present, nothing else. We turned our guest bedroom into a meditation room and that's where we sit in a row. My husband is resistant but does it for Leo, and also because we have a follow-up meeting with Dr. Stevens in three months and I think my husband is afraid of Dr. Stevens. I don't mean afraid in a physical sense—my husband is a big man—but in more of a psychological sense. It's like Dr. Stevens is the father and the three of us are his children. One time when the three of us took the one seat and tried out the mountain meditation, where you get an image of a mountain in your head and breathe into the image and concentrate on your breath until the image of the mountain and your body become one, Leo got up from his seat and banged his hand against the wall and mumbled angry things I couldn't quite understand except to know that they were angry, and then my husband got up from his seat—gladly, I think—to try to calm Leo, but I stayed where I was, I remained still and rooted because a mountain is still and rooted no matter what happens to or around it, I remained mindful of everything that was happening around me, even Leo not listening to my husband and my husband saying, Well, suit yourself then! See where breaking your own hand will get you! When this kind of thing happens, when I feel the world around me falling apart, I try to breathe in this feeling, I try to embrace it, not run away from it. I try to become a witness and nothing but. I practice dying on purpose and letting the world go on without me. I notice a thought that says, Get up! Do something! Then I laugh inside myself and say, Don't just do something! Sit there! I focus on my cosmic *mudra*—my hands together in my lap, the fingers of one hand lying atop the fingers of the other, my thumb tips gently touching as if circling an invisible egg I must not break or allow to be broken, but must not be afraid to break or allow to be broken. Sometimes I notice a thought about blame. I want to place blame on someone. On my son, my husband, anyone, the world. But where do you place blame? And what is the world? Am I not part of the world? Are you not? So we sit together, the mountain and me, until only the mountain remains.

2.2

—The reason I'm not sleeping at home tonight is simple. My

wife punched the dog. She actually made a fist and punched the dog. So I took the dog and came to my office and pulled out the couch.

—I don't know where he is, but he left here the way he did to make me feel like a monster. He comforted the dog and kept saying, It's okay. I won't let anyone hurt you anymore. You're safe now. Then he put on his coat and said, I trust you not to harm my child while I'm gone. Imagine him being protective of his child! He's not fooling anyone. If it were up to him, my God—the way he lets our daughter run near the stairs.

—The dog yelped, her ears went back, and then she ran into her crate with her tail between her legs. When I called her out of her crate, she wouldn't come. When I went to get her out, she backed away from me all the way to the back of the crate.

—The dog is fine.

—It would break my heart to see such a big dog flinch when you raise your hand to give her a typical command like sit. One thing I loved about our first dog—the one we had to put down—was that she wasn't afraid of anything except thunder and lightning. You could walk over her and put your foot down near her face and she wouldn't flinch. You could reach for the rubber bone in her mouth and sometimes by accident whack her in the eye and even then she'd come right back at you. Now my fear is that our new dog, which it took us so many hours of discussion to even decide to get—after what happened with Newman—will become afraid of even her owners' hands raised. Once a dog is afraid of something like that, how do you get her to not be afraid? I'm not sure you can. Or at least it would take a lot of work and retraining. I'm not a psychologist, but I imagine it's the same with a kid who gets hit. I don't believe in hitting, period. Unless hitting someone is the only way to save your life or theirs—let's say your kid is about to touch a wall socket or something—then, sure, you might whack the kid's hand. But that's for protection.

—I'm not taking any chances. If it's your child, you can do whatever you want. But with my child, I don't take chances. I know the kinds of things that can happen.

—There was absolutely no reason for it. The dog was just being a dog. Our daughter had a piece of cheese in her hand and the dog was sniffing the cheese and licking it, and our daughter was laughing, she was having fun, the dog's tongue was tickling our daughter's hand, and then the dog started nibbling the cheese, which our daughter was now holding near her own face, so from a certain angle, with the dog's mouth moving the way it was, it might have seemed like something not so good was going on, but for God's sake, take a look before you punch, make sure what you're doing before you do it. I mean, we know this dog—we've had her now for almost two years—and she's never been anything but super-sweet with everyone, people and other dogs and especially with kids, and I realize what happened with Newman and how difficult that was, but just because something happened once doesn't mean it's going to happen again. But people tend to think the opposite—that if something happened once, it'll happen again. Just like if you hit someone, the next time you raise your hand, even to say hello or point out something, the person you hit—or maybe someone else hit—might flinch or turn away. But think about it, it makes more sense, doesn't it, that if something happens—especially something as unexpected as what happened with Newman—the chance of the same thing happening is pretty low, I'd say. It's kind of like getting struck by lightning. If I ever get struck by lightning, I suppose I might become afraid to be outside during a lightning storm. But a more rational response might be to be less afraid of lightning storms because what are the chances, right.

—The dog's a dog. She'll survive getting hit in the face once, and I did not punch her, my hand was not closed into a fist, that's simply not true.

—Her name is Toby, which is short for her full name, October, which is our favorite month.

—My husband pushed hard for the dog. To be honest, I think he uses the dog as a distraction from being a husband and father. It's easy to own a dog, especially after the dog's trained. You can put the dog in her crate and not think about her. With a baby, it's not so easy. Sophia is almost three, so she's running around, she's talking, she's getting into things. She has to be watched all the time.

—I'm sorry, I thought you meant the dog's name. Sophie. That's what I like to call her, but my wife corrects me and says, Her name is Sophia. I want her to know her full name. Sometimes, I swear, I don't know.

—I think it's pretty telling that he left with the dog. That's the way I see this family—as two families. One is me and Sophia, the other is him and the dog. I see it whenever something difficult comes up. Like most recently Sophia being embarrassed of and not understanding her lisp, which one of her friends made fun of. All I wanted to do was to talk about it as a family, for the two of us to sit down with our daughter and reassure her, but as soon as Sophia started to cry my husband whistled—so quietly that he tried to deny ever having done it—and in runs the dog right to my husband, and they proceeded to play tug o' war with that goddamn rubber bone while we were discussing our daughter's lisp. Some people might not think that's a big deal, but I know he whistled because he was uncomfortable with the conversation, it was getting too serious for him, he actually had to be a father. This is what he does when he's stressed or uncomfortable—he focuses his attention on the dog. Other people smoke or drink or eat too much, but my husband babies the dog. It's all the same thing.

—I wanted to get another dog because it's relaxing. It helps ground me. Even going for a walk early in the morning and watching her sniff other dog's pee. Sounds silly, but I get pleasure from watching the dog just be a dog. It helps get rid of all the clutter in my head.

—On the weekends he walks the dog five, sometimes six times a day. Now you show me a dog that really needs to be walked that many times in a day.

—The other reason is that if we wanted a dog but didn't get one just because of what happened with Newman, then that would be a victory for fear.

—It had nothing to do with Newman. But let's just say, for argument's sake, that it did. If we don't learn from the past, then what good is the past?

—Give me a break—it's been over three years and she still calls that boy on his birthday and asks the boy's mother how his face looks and how noticeable the scarring still is. I mean, the first year I got on the phone and spoke to the kid, asked him how he was doing, what he got for his birthday, but after three years, you have to let it go. Now when she calls and tries to put me on the phone, I say no, and of course we get into a fight about it. She tells me that they appreciate our call, but I would bet my last dollar that those people don't want us calling anymore; they just want to put the incident behind them, which clearly my wife hasn't been able to do.

—When I ask him about his childhood, he shrugs and says, It was fine. I don't know what else to say. It was fine. He and I both know what kind of a man his father was—he was very strict and borderline cold—and sometimes I just want to know what that was like for my husband, I want to hear what he struggled with, what he was afraid of—intimate details from his life before I knew him. But all he can say is, I don't understand what you want to know. It was fine. Even the incident with Newman—he doesn't want to talk about it. Once, I caught him smelling the dog's ashes, which we keep in a box in the basement, and he said, I thought I smelled something funny, and I wanted to make sure a mouse didn't get into the box and die. We both knew that was made up. Me, I think about what happened, of course I do. The way that mother screamed. I have nightmares about it. Sometimes I wake and it's me screaming.

—In the morning and probably into the afternoon we'll have a marathon session of trying to work through this, where my wife will tell me for the umpteenth time that I need to be in therapy, and I will explain to her that I don't need to be in therapy and I should know because I'm me, and no one knows me better than me.

—I don't think it's very responsible for him to leave like this. What if, I don't know, what if there's some kind of emergency with Sophia and we need to get her to a hospital—let's say she swallows a button—and he has the car? Whose conscience is that going to be on?

—This will blow over. These things always do. But it's a sign that something bigger isn't right. I'm not sure how we're going to fix that bigger thing.

—For example, for Christmas he gave his daughter three books she already has. He gave the dog a new rubber bone even though the old rubber bone was just fine.

1.2

FINAL REPORT OF THE INDEPENDENT COMMITTEE TO REVIEW

SUCH MATTERS AS HAVE BEEN OUTLINED

Based on evidence provided by numerous witnesses, reporters, sub- and sub-sub-committees, and national and international organizations, we are unable to determine conclusively whether or not the events and activities as outlined above actually occurred. Available testimony does not necessarily point conclusively to any alleged abuses. It is the policy of this committee that the testimony of any alleged victim must be corroborated by extensive and reliable testimony by nonpartisan witnesses conclusively unrelated by blood or otherwise to the alleged victim and/or by confessions obtained legally from alleged assailants and/or incontrovertible evidence such as video footage proven to be real and not doctored or DNA evidence proven to be real and not doctored. If there is even a reasonable doubt as to the authenticity of either witness testimony or alleged assailant confession or physical evidence, that testimony or confession or physical evidence must be thrown away as if it never existed. Concerning the events and activities under investigation, only circumstantial evidence has been obtained by this committee and its sub- and sub-sub committees. This committee is not prepared at this time to declare the alleged assailants conclusively guilty of the charges brought against them. We are not prepared to use the word guilty, nor the word conclusive, in relation to the charges. We would need to obtain more conclusive non-doctored/non-partisan evidence in order to use either the word guilty or conclusive. For now, we will stick with the words circumstantial and inconclusive. Perhaps if we had video footage of the alleged biting incident, or the alleged pinching incident, or the alleged use of a log to allegedly beat the alleged victim to the point at which she allegedly expired, perhaps then we might be willing to consider using the words possibly conclusive, or at least to use the word inconclusive less conclusively. Beyond video footage of the alleged victim being bitten, pinched, and beaten with a log, or beyond the alleged assailant coming forward without being coerced and confessing to the allegations in question, we have no choice but to continue using the words we've been using. There have been witnesses, we admit, but all of these witnesses allege that their wives and husbands and parents and children and brothers and sisters have also been victims of the alleged assailant and his alleged soldiers, and so we must declare these witnesses partisan and disregard their testimony. Photographs of the alleged dead are not considered conclusive evidence because these photographs are static and might prove that a body has expired, but nothing beyond that. We have found no record of anyone using the name Kony or Selindi or Ali Salango or Jim Rickey or Who Are You, and it is entirely possible that such names are mythical in nature, names passed along from generation to generation much in the way ghost stories are passed along, or urban myths, around a campfire. Though we have obtained hundreds of pages of testimony and hundreds of photographs of bodies that have expired, we are not prepared at this time to declare conclusively that the alleged incidents and practices as outlined above have been conclusively proven in the conclusive manner necessary for us to be conclusive in declaring such practices as having conclusively occurred. If the committee obtains enough conclusive evidence, the committee might be willing to declare at some point that it might be possible that such practices might be occurring, and we might be willing to upgrade the status of such possible happenings from possible to possibly probable. In the spirit of knowing the truth, and in the spirit of spending your taxpayer dollars wisely, the committee fully welcomes any further evidence that might help us upgrade the possible to the possibly probable, though we must remind you that it would take a substantial amount of conclusive non-partisan testimony and/or non-doctored evidence and/or non-coerced confessions for us to even consider maybe upgrading from possible to possibly probable. And even if we do upgrade to possibly probable, we would need to form another sub-committee to investigate whether the possibly probable might possibly be upgraded to the possibly likely, and even if that sub-committee upgrades to possibly likely, that sub-committee would need to form a sub-sub-committee to determine whether the possibly likely might possibly be upgraded to probably likely, and even then, that sub-sub-committee would need to form a sub-sub-sub-committee to determine if the probably likely might possibly be upgraded to very nearly likely, which is not yet even likely, let alone conclusive. And even if one of the many sub-committees came back to this main committee using the word conclusive, we would have to form another sub-committee to determine what, if anything, should be done. In the meantime, the committee would like to remind you that there are laws.

Our nation has laws, the world has laws, and, most importantly, the Almighty has laws. It should comfort you, we hope, that people have been instructed to adhere to the law, and we trust that they do so. You might look at the many laws we have on the books; they might provide comfort for you. If this comfort is not a comfort for you, let us offer you an even greater comfort: the certainty, or fair certainty, that what happens elsewhere, especially on the other side of the globe, especially inside a human body that is not your body, that does not look like your body, will not affect us here, where we are preparing this report, where you are reading it. If this comfort is not a comfort to you, if you are one of those people who believe that what happens there happens here, what happens here happens there, what happens anywhere happens everywhere, then perhaps the report you're looking for is beyond the concerns, is beyond the obligations of this committee.

THE LUCKY ONE'S GET TO BE PEOPLE BY RACHEL HALEY HIMMELHEBER

THE LUCKY ONES
GET TO BE PEOPLE

by Rachel Haley Himmelheber

WHAT WE ARE is bodies, I want to tell him. Bodies. Bodies, bodies. Fucking is as good a way as any to be alive. What does it matter that we are in this airport? What does it matter that we are in this airport together? What matters is that we are drinking lemonade, that water and artificial lemon flavor and refined sugar are traveling the short boulevard of my throat, that I will swallow this liquid, transform it, rid myself of it, and try again.

I'm fucking my retarded neighbor. His name is Rich, and he lives in 2A. I live in 11B, upstairs and around the corner. He's closer to the laundry room. We've been together three weeks.

After I kissed him the first time, I thought I'd be able to hate him soon. I thought his voice would bug me or maybe he'd spit or drool. But he doesn't disgust me.

His apartment looks like the apartment of a homosexual man. His sofa print is cabbage roses. The wood is dark and polished, and he owns a tea set. His china is blue and grown-up sized. I had a yellow set when I was ten. I love to have tea parties with him. He lets me pour.

"What kind of tea, Rich?" I call from the kitchen. It's been overcast for a month now, the sky the dull gray of ashes. Afternoons, the sun is out for thirty minutes and then it disappears. Rich doesn't want to have sex all the time, which makes him different from other inappropriate decisions I've made.

"You choose," he says. "Earl Grey? You choose."

He has only two kinds: Earl Grey and Jasmine. I am bored. "You left the stove on, Rich. That's dangerous," I say. Rich did not leave the stove on, but I bend to turn all four knobs on and then off, as if he had. Rich is afraid of fire. He has three rooms and three smoke detectors.

He is suddenly behind me. "I know how to do things right," he says. "I turn the stove off."

I am already tired. "You're just forgetful, Rich." I take the cream from the refrigerator. "I do it, too."

"You do?"

"Sure. Sometimes." Never, actually, but I might if I used my stove.

"Janie?" Rich asks. "You're not retarded?" He is a suspicious man. If he weren't, his retardation would bug me more. Suspicion must indicate some kind of intelligence.

I kiss him, my fingers gripping his doughy back.

There is a whole universe under the stalagmites and stalactites, a wizard and a joker and a queen under the upended cave. Walking—even on the lighted, benign paths—feels unsafe, like being cupped in the palm of someone you don't trust; the lines on the palm become huge overwhelming cracks that, path or no path, I could fall into. I can't help but want the deep fall; the bottom isn't present because it's so darkly lit. The little lights and the one green Wrigley's wrapper only add to the feeling of wildness, wildness on a thin border of civilization, the veneer of tame and domestic human animals stretching taut the further and further I see into the darkness. Looking at the crystals and dripping pieces of rock, my teeth come alive: I feel fiberglass between them, a squeaky itch, like the slight crack of millions and millions of baby toes ground to a pulpy mess. In the jutted points and hollowed out deepness, I feel like I've walked inside my own body; I am traveling through my ear canal—and I can walk forever.

I tell Rich about the caverns because it's his favorite story and because I can make him see the formations—the icy Christmas trees and the breasts covered with sugar frosting and the popcorn clusters and the pencils. I am a good storyteller. But mostly I like to tell him about the caverns because everything in them is phallic: purposeful spears of stalagmite piercing the stalactites. I always wanted to climb on them. I always wanted to disturb everything. "That's nature, Janie," said my mother, holding me by my arm as if nature were something sacred that I was not permitted to interrupt.

I throw away faxes, hang up on phone calls as soon as I'm on hold, misdirect mail, file out of order. I'm going to get fired eventually, but this place is one of those places where you're lucky if they notice that you punch in and punch out, sit there all day, collect a paycheck every other week. They don't care.

Rich comes to borrow something. I'm in my towel, watching him knock on doors up and down.

Sunlight is slanting through the peephole. It lights Rich up; his hair looks like the fur of a ginger cat.

I know who Rich is because the maintenance man told me about him when I moved in. "There's a retard on the first floor. Harmless guy. Watches out his window all day. Might come ask you your name."

"Should I tell him?" (I think there are rules.)

"Sure, if you want. His name's Rich. He pays in cash," the maintenance man said. "He's cool."

"I'm sorry," Rich says, averting his eyes from my toweled body.

We both look down. I have beautiful toes. They are painted purple.

"Would you like to come in?" I shut the door as I move backwards.

His mouth is funny to kiss. I've never kissed a woman, but his lips feel like a woman's. He lets me lead. His body is soft, too, soft in the way a woman's is soft. Male fat is still hard somehow, no matter how overweight the man.

I treat each wart differently. I have two—both on my thumb. My favorite way to treat them is to use the wart remover pad for several days exactly the way it's prescribed and then play with the wart. Salicylic acid on the brown dot on the pad; it looks like a round Band-Aid, but I know that, underneath, acid is eating my thumb.

The warts are thicker than skin—like a blister, except not fragile. No one notices them, I know, because no one looks that closely. It's hard to keep the pads on for 48 hours—they get wet and fall off. I've rectified this situation somewhat by wrapping surgical tape around the pads. After I've left them for 48 hours, I take my first peek at the wart. It's no longer smooth; it looks like a miniature head of cauliflower, and sometimes, if I'm lucky, I can see the black pieces under the whites of skin: the roots from which the wart is growing, a whole evil kingdom beneath a sparkling salt castle.

"I'm sorry," Rich says. "I know you're not retarded."

I don't care. "Get the sugar," I say. "I have the cream." The cream is crusty, hardened edges on the soggy cardboard flaps, and the liquid inside, sloshing voluptuously in its blue container, strikes me as unreal.

"Mother's mad," he says to himself, half singing the words. "Mother's mad, Mother's mad."

He calls me Mother, although not usually to my face. I called my college boyfriend Daddy, but only in bed. Rich doesn't call me anything in bed; I think Mother is supposed to be a joke of some kind, an attempt at sarcasm. I wouldn't care if he called me Mother in bed. It'd be like a promotion.

I say, "Never mind, Rich. I know where the sugar is. You can go watch TV."

The tea is ready, but I don't want it anymore. Rich's apartment is the same as mine, but it looks different. He has furniture upholstered in roses. When I'd lived here two months, I realized my stuff didn't work in this new apartment. I wanted something spartan, something empty to sit in the center of. What I didn't sell or give to the woman next door I broke. I threw a lot of glass around and then bagged it. My calves are still cut from the sliced plastic banging against me.

Rich is sitting on the cabbage roses, his feet in a patch of sun on the shag carpet. He's watching the news with a fiercely concentrated stare. I feel like kissing the back of his freckled neck and at the same time throwing the hot tea on his spongy head. I turn the left front burner knob back to HIGH and around again to OFF, testing the feeling in my fingers. If the building were to burn down, everyone, including Rich, would believe it's his fault. Even I wouldn't believe I'd done it.

I sit next to him on the roses. "Why are you sad?" he asks.

"I want to be near other people," I say.

"We can go to the airport," he says. On the screen, a reporter gestures in front of the wreckage of a downed plane. "You want to go?"

"Okay," I say.

Our first time isn't great. Rich comes in less than a minute, but I'm pretty sure he's a virgin. He does whatever I tell him to and, grateful, I believe he will remember for next time. Improvement will be steady.

I explain details. Indirect pressure here; soft, soft; three fingers just there; your head should tilt more; no, less; perfect; yes. I feel like a doctor. Scalpel, please, nurse. This sex is precise and precisely enjoyable. Clinical but well executed. Technically, I know I am having a worthwhile experience, but I also know I can never let myself go. I know because my eyes are always open and because of the clarity with which I can measure distance and pleasure.

It's always cold in Boston. I'm always cold. My professor has a hairy blond back and he tries to read my newspaper mornings in bed.

I used to be a history major. People in Boston are all ages; that's what makes me want to go to North Carolina—I want everybody to be the same age and everywhere I go everyone to have the same face. The stores will sell the same products to everyone. In Boston, the people I meet are capable of anything and the world is full of possibility; there's ethnic food and the airport with people coming and going. I want to talk to the cashier at the grocery store and use the same words. I want to say the same words to everyone. I have no desire to create unique relationships. I can't imagine why I ever did.

I work with all women. I went to apply in my blue suit with my maroon faux-leather resume holder. Blue low-heeled pumps. Lipstick. Dressed-up stupid like a doll. We all wear jeans to work. I was hired immediately.

At lunch, Toni talks the most. These other women remind me of animals. I try to use the men's bathroom whenever possible because there's something about these women—their fat white asses in their flowered underwear, warm and soft, and I don't need to be communal about that—their smells and their insides. They hum while they take a shit. I don't care.

Toni talks about big issues—diapers, abortion, evolution. I make jokes. They think I'm a card, but sometimes there's an awkward silence. They know I try to be funny, and no one can bring herself to think of this impulse as ungenerous, malicious.

"Well, I for one believe we evolved," says Toni biting into her sandwich. "A lot of men haven't finished the process."

Laughter.

Her sandwich is the gummy-white-bread-mayo-processed-cheese-bologna kind, and I want it. I'm not eating much, and I'm rarely hungry.

"A lot?" I ask, mock-shocked. "All the men I know, Toni,"

I say, and the rest of the girls agree. I smile because I feel dangerous, as if I could keep these women even if they don't keep me.

This china figurine is pink and gray and baby blue. For something that's hollow inside, it's surprisingly solid. It has the weight of my mother's expectations, of my childhood ballet classes, of every locker room I've ever been in, every naked body I've ever touched. I've smashed everything else, and I can't ignore that this one is different, that I hold it a little longer. I want to feel the pink girl smash; if I could open these fragile accumulated pieces on my head, I would. People crack walnuts on their heads, smash beer cans in fists, karate chop wood with outstretched sides of palms. If only someone had told me that so much mess could be so satisfying, had let me break dishes—just once, break a dish instead of a lifetime of washing carefully, scraping, soaking, drying, putting away tidily.

I climb in the bathtub first. Rich stands and watches me lower myself. His stare is so male, I forget he's retarded. My legs are partially exposed, and I try to splash it over me, but it's heavy. Lotion doesn't flow; it settles.

"What are you doing," Rich asks, "wiggling like that?"

I look at my legs, pale and unshaven, scabs in various states of being. "Just get in or leave."

Rich takes his clothes off and gets in, adjusts his head around the faucet and his legs around me. His stomach is the stomach of a boy at the beach in June: hairless and eager after the long cold. I search for something on his body that is a man's rather than a boy's.

The lotion is sloppy: gummy and creamy, a potion of clotted cream and sperm and the spots that signify strep throat. I think about how to clean out the tub. The lotion won't drain well. I imagine explaining to the maintenance man.

"Would you clean the tub out for me later?" I ask Rich. I picture the big sloppy bag, pulsing with lotion, hoisted over his sloping shoulder.

"Sure," he says, reaching his unpracticed hand to grab my thigh.

I must need this kind of groping, I think, because it feels good.

I drive everywhere because Rich doesn't have a driver's license. I don't know if he could pass the test. He can read, and he knows the signs. I don't mind driving; we rarely go out.

He is dressed in hat and gloves and scarf. He offers to rub my bare hands in his, but I like them cold. I signal to the other drivers that I am turning into the short-term parking. The airport feels like the biggest place in the world because, I think, of its formidable front. Airports are always long and surrounded by blank air, so they give the illusion of grandeur even if they're puny. The Asheville airport has only two terminals. I choose gate A2 because the most people are there.

Rich wants to sit in the Starbucks near the entrance, but once I explain about the metal detectors, he agrees with me.

"It's safer," I say. "No one can bring anything bad into this part of the airport. In Starbucks, anyone can bring guns or knives or bombs. We're better off."

"Stop pinching my arm," he says. "I want to go home."

He makes me angry when he's a baby. "Let's just walk through the metal detectors, get a drink, and then I'll let you go home."

The professor and I live in a nice apartment: lots of furniture, silver bowls, fistfuls of plums to put in the bowls, books books books. I'm in love with the original wood floors. I stay awake at night, way past when the professor has murmured and snored his way to sleep. He sleeps deeply, and I used to watch him, the moving of his eyes under their vulnerable lids, the way his smell changes as he goes deeper into rest. But now all I want is to be by myself, to see myself only. I build a barrier in our bed with the extra pillows, silky-edged fabric with an ironed feel— the sheets and pillowcases are so expensive that they feel both soft and crisp. I sit and press to change the color of the inside of my eyelids. I press on the edges and gradually work the pads of my thumbs to the center of my eyes. I push until I can follow that actual tunnel behind them where all of the colors bleed. At the end of the tunnel is an expanse: uncharted territory and wide-open spaces. How far can you fall inside your own head? I travel as far as I can then I let go and sleep. As with any other purging of the body, I feel better afterwards.

I buy utilitarian North Carolina groceries I don't usually eat and toiletries at Ingles and Wal-Mart and sit on my apartment floor. I have shag carpet and I like to thread my toes through the strands of fiber and lay on my back. I pretend it's a field and I have wind in the fan and sun in the light. I have to spend my paychecks, regular as rain, every two weeks a new one, and there's nothing to buy. I don't want to save them. I don't want food, I don't want drinks or dancing or movies or drugs or clothes or books. I like the tea parties with Rich, and if I put cream and sugar in my blue cup, I'm nourished. The girls at work are rolling in fat; their asses push up when they sit on the chairs—it forms a sort of wall on their backs, and they pull their pleated jeans past the point of their bulk. The professor had a paunch, a slight ripply area that I would lay my head against while I laughed at the TV. I'm so thin now; the girls at work say I disappear if I turn sideways. Practically all I drink is cream, the thicker the better, there's no reason to diet I say to the girls. Just to make them mad. It's all about your state of mind. If you want to be thin and you love cream, drink it. Leaning over to cup a part of Toni, one of the parts it's polite to touch, a love handle or an upper arm pillow, I squeeze slowly, so Toni will be left wondering why she always feels I'm hostile when I am nothing but kind gestures and goodwill. She will question her own prejudices. Janie is a good girl. Why do I think so poorly of people? What's wrong with me?

When I stare at babies, I smile and flirt because the mom likes that; then, when I can, I narrow my eyes and try to burn a feeling of hate into the baby. It's amazingly easy to do. If I turn the ceiling fan on, the plastic Ingles bags fly around, trying to grab and choke me. The tall and empty walls look transparent sometimes, like I could walk through them if I knew the password.

On the bar, a jar of pickled eggs swims in cloudy vinegar; I want to touch their silky, resilient surface. Eggs in vinegar are to regular hard-boiled eggs what sea-polished stones are to ordinary stones: a valuable, sensual difference, an object you want to hold and hold and roll your naked body all over. People do get massages with heated wet sea stones. I try to picture Toni with pickled eggs, a handsome foreign man rubbing the ovals all over her. Suddenly, the eggs crack and the foreign man rubs the chalky yolks into her skin, mashing and mashing the pungent bite of the yellow; arched shoulder blades and soft recesses, secret hidden places filmed over with egg. Humpty Dumpty sat on a wall, Humpty Dumpty exploded his contents on her naked back. I laugh, and the girls stop talking and look at me. I must be more careful; I must know what makes me laugh before noise erupts from me. I pretend to sip at my beer; the girls are too drunk to notice how little I've had.

The Town Pump is my favorite bar: dollar bills flap on the ceiling with thumbtacks, you have to throw it up hard enough so that the bill stays in, small room, tables crammed, tiny tables for two, four people at a table is too much—the tables are round, I've always thought a masochistic claustrophobic would love it here. Would fall in love here. Wood walls with metal beer signs, PBR on tap, the bar runs along the left side of the wall; the bathroom is nasty. The sopping wet corners of toilet paper, the rusty fringe on the white metal pop-up lid of the trashcan, its foot beckons me to pop up, pop up, but everyone throws the trash on the floor. Old people drink here—mountain men and their women; I'm almost to the railroad tracks, to the pretend train caboose thing that sits there—it was the tourist agency but now it's a Beanie Baby Xmas store, down and to the right is the Black Mountain Goodwill, the time and temperature on the bank sign are never correct, it's not important, the ice cream shops and the sawdust left from carvings for rich people tourists, Have it shipped to us, I imagine them saying, their arms already full to spillover of ceramic pieces and subtly flowered bags, but they're not here: it's strictly a local bar. When I walk out, it's a postcard of purple breathing and lit edges of billboards against the Blue Ridge sky. The sudden air from the claustrophobia to the open mountains on Cherry Street shocks me every time.

The bathtub has so many toys in it that I can't put my head under without encountering one floating by. I skim under the water level just enough so that I can breathe through the tip of my nose. It's so warm! My mother spanked me earlier because I told the whole ballet class we were buying a big mansion with candles on all the walls and a five car garage and a swimming pool, and she came behind me and spanked me in front of everyone and now I'm going to drown in this warm bathtub.

She left me in the bath all by myself after I told her I was going to drown. My behind stopped tingling before I got in the bath but it hurt for a long time because I just had my leotard and my tights on.

In the bathtub, it's hard to remember what came first. Under the water, there's a new sound I can hear, and I try to forget ballet class, and I can, but my mother's big mouth appears unless I shut my eyes and sink my head all the way down.

My hair is blond at the tips and as silky as Rapunzel's. It's better in the water than when I suck on the tips of my braids. I like how silky it is and how it threads through the water. If I sit up, it changes back into regular old hair, but under the water, it's better than a crown, better than a cashmere hat.

The hallway smells like celery and sage and cinnamon. The door closes with a sort of swoosh: something to do with the warmth and the cold wind.

"Janie?" calls my mother from the kitchen's laughter. "Is that you?"

Spilling out from the stove and the refrigerator and the counters are a bunch of her AA friends. My mother's new family. Her just-finished kitchen has stools and a bar-table-thing and everyone is chopping and kissing and exclaiming and stuffing olives and spoons of mashed potatoes in my face. My mother hugs me.

"She took a taxicab back from the bus station," my mother explains to all her stupid friends. "She made the trip by herself so we could cook. Isn't that amazing?"

Oh, they were certain something would work out, such a smart capable girl, just look at your mother, just look at this kitchen, all redecorated by herself and how could a pretty girl like me not have a steady guy, was I just studying too hard?

"It's a shame at the holidays especially," I say, searching for what could be cruel, what could be wistful, how much I could risk, and how much I could pay, "that I have no father."

My mother's AA friends all fall silent, each thinking, I am sure, of the different story my mother has manufactured about who my father is and why he is not here with me at Thanksgiving.

Driving to work is the best part of my days—the straight lines of the highway to Hendersonville or the winding of the Parkway. I'm on 25 now and I just passed the drive-thru deli and I'm hungry. I haven't been hungry. U-turn and the man at the drive-thru wears a little hat.

When I bite into the sandwich with its funny toasted bread, a chunk of turkey falls on my wrist and I lick it off and taste salt and I think of biting into the blue vein, the smooshy one that I can push around and spread my blood all over my turkey and Swiss. I'm in the parking lot, bolting the sandwich before I'm late. I want to tell the girls about Rich. But not retarded Rich. Rich. A rich man. He has lots of cars and he buys me fancy desserts and bottles of wine with dinner at the Grove Park last night and when they squeal I'll look coy and they'll all know I'm fucking him and Toni will say, "You've got a real glow about you, Janie," which is girl code for happiness.

"You'll have a little girl someday and then you'll understand," my mother says, giving my hair a final twist.

I imagine my little girl as a doll, name her Rose Emily, play with her; I don't tell her when she's bad because she's never bad and I'm never bad either.

"Tell about the cave," Rich says. "Did you climb on the mountains, Janie?"

"Yes, after my mother stopped looking, I did." I didn't actually, but it's a better story if I did, and I am able to describe it well. "Deep underground, there was a different world, round as Earth. It had winding paths lit with colored lights and they shone on my bare ankles as I climbed. They were like mountains, but craggy, slippery mountains. The water looked like it would make the caverns slimy but that was just an illusion of the colored lights. Really, everything was warm and comfortable, once you reached a point high enough to not get caught."

"How did they make you come down?" Rich asks. He loves this part.

"Well, my mother turned into this evil witch and it was like I was a princess in a tower, a castle tower with crystal walls way down deep in a mine."

"Like God's house," Rich says sagely.

"What?"

"You know, like if God built houses."

"Exactly," I continue. "And she went to get a policeman to help her catch me and put me back in captivity, but I put a spell on everyone visiting the caverns that day and instead of trying to get me down, everyone came to look at me perched on this big glittering mound. I became the attraction, a princess in a tower. And when I got tired I came down and went to eat at the coffee shop with my mother. We both had chicken salad sandwiches."

"Your favorite," Rich says, touching my left breast with his palm in a wondering way. A way that seems more suited to touching a piece of art. The Rosetta Stone or the Vietnam Wall where your dad's name is, a way that honors and that uses every nerve in the palm of your hand.

"Right," I say. "And then we went home and had a happy life forever and ever after."

We fuck right there on the floor and usually I try to pay attention, honest I do, but this time, looking at the swirled texture of Rich's plaster ceiling, all I can think of is how I used to be positive that God was talking to me. Clouds moving meant one thing, bells ringing another. When I was in fifth grade, there was a solar eclipse, and I believed that meant something really big, that all wars would end or my father would come back or the world would die in a nuclear explosion. I would be the only person forewarned, whatever came to pass.

When Rich sees the bathtub, he is curious. I'd filled the bathtub with lotion. Eight family-sized bottles. I did it for my skin—my skin cracks in these mountains; there's no more give to it; it breaks. I bleed sometimes. I bought nine bottles, but eight was enough to fill the bottom of the tub. I knew before I started that it wasn't going to be full.

I give him the cracked soles of my feet to hold. I recognize that I am operating in a sort of trance; there is a distinct feeling in me that nothing is permanent, that I can erase this, too, later.

"I have to go," he says. He has an erection.

I grab his body with my feet and pull him in. "Stay," I say, not caring how I sound.

I'm turning my coffee cup around and around to watch the liquid, luxurious with thick cream, coat the sides of my oversized mug. I'm looking at the coffee to keep from looking at him, this blond professor from BU, this first person who's flirted with me in Boston.

"What do you consider," he asks, his piercing blue eyes looking at my coffee's movement, "the most defining experience of your adolescence?"

Men like this, I think, are the reason I love Boston. Smart men must care more about you; their simplest questions betray their caring.

"Here is what I remember," I say. "It's about ballet

class. I was twelve, just starting to grow into my decidedly non-ballerina type body. I was starting pointe shoes that day, which is a very big deal. It meant many more hours a week, more dedication. In the changing room, the older girls tried to scare me before I tried on my new pointe shoes; I knew they were only trying to scare me, but it still worked a little bit."

He's still interested, and his eyes have a liquid look, so I keep chattering about the ballet girls.

The professor is staring at me as if I'm the most interesting and wonderful person he's ever met. "Janie, right?"

I nod, but he knows it's my name because he continues.

"Why is it that such a smart and gifted young woman is satisfied with having coffee alone on such a beautiful morning? Could someone convince you to perhaps join him for an early lunch?"

"Oh, well," I say. "I'm just spending time alone. I don't really think I could be convinced."

"I'll bet," he says, leaning closer, "that this old person could convince you in no time."

On my back under the table, I decide I'm tired of pretending that the table is a spaceship. My legs won't reach the top, so I rest them on the smooth polished curve of the leg. I'm sleepy.

I dream: A man my mother calls my father is naked and crying. My mother takes her sewing scissors to his boy part and slashes him and slashes him and he bleeds and cries. His hair is blond like the tips of my braids. My mother's hair is brown like the tops of my braids. She is so angry. He looks like the man who plays piano at ballet and then he looks like Mr. Bryce the gym teacher. My mother calls him Janie's dad. Janie's dad is crying and holding himself, but there isn't blood anymore.

I've stopped paying attention. There are no windows in BU classrooms. My pencil drums a name over and over again between the lines of blue on my page, between the professor's eyes. Rasputin. Rasputin. Rasputin. Russian history doesn't even count for me anymore unless I want to make it my concentration. You're supposed to stop fucking around and specialize. But I can't decide what's important, what's interesting. Everything and nothing. "You want too much," my mother always said, as if that were a desire I could will into submission.

My legs are scaly. The stupid podunk North Carolina weatherman is always saying the humidity is high, and I think of sending pictures of my legs to Channel 7. Are these the legs of someone who lives in a wet climate? I can see the newscasters and producers and writers standing around the photo. Heck, no! they'd think. These are the legs of a girl in trouble! The weatherman would be fired, and they'd hire me. I'd be the new hero, the weather girl who tells it like it is. People everywhere would send special creams and lotions.

The scales remind me of my grandmother's liver-spotted arms, wrinkled and soft like a tissue that's been used and wrung, folded and crinkled and stuffed into a pocketbook and left to dry. I'm too young for my legs. Their skin feels divorced from the rest of me, as if someone left me his old used-up skin and took my firm flesh. The scales disappear with lotion, but it's like invisible ink: it resurfaces.

Rich is pouting. "I want coffee," he whines. "A mocha."

"Are you paying?"

A wordless shaking of his head.

"I didn't think so. Next time, Rich, if you remember your wallet, you can choose the drinks. But I want lemonade and I want us both to drink the same thing."

There are lemons floating in the glass pitcher and it's February but warm in the airport and just the idea of lemonade is hopeful.

"I moved to North Carolina for porch swings and lemonade," I say. "Do you understand, Rich?"

"There's stuff you want that you don't get," he says, and I nod. I don't know if he's right or not, but it feels good to have somebody else name this feeling.

Toni's husband will take us home if we get too drunk. Her husband isn't particularly handsome or smart, but she can brag about him to us, and he can drive. The jukebox is playing Willie Nelson and I have a sudden urge to take off my clothes and dance naked on one of the crowded tables. Sloppy naked, scattering beer bottles with the turn of my foot. I'll do an Irish jig. At BU, a girl walked out in the courtyard of the dorms and announced that she wanted to have sex. It wasn't a stampede or anything, but there were definitely takers. Could I fuck any of the dispirited looking men in here? I'm sure their wives look like Toni—fat asses retaining the elastic outline of their underwear long after the underwear's been discarded. My neglected but trim ass would be a welcome relief.

"I've got a new boyfriend," I say to the group, turning the beer in my glass until it sloshes over the side. "He's great in bed."

The man asks, "You want insurance?"

"What do you recommend?" I ask.

The man looks surprised. "Well, of course, I recommend it. Except—well, yeah, I recommend it. Very important. Where are you moving again?"

"North Carolina."

"Oh, yeah. Long drive. Insurance would be the smart thing to do. You can return this baby at any U-Haul dealer. You pay by the day."

"What else do I need?"

"Um, do you need pads? You know, to cushion valuables? We sell straps and all sorts of cushioning and restraints."

Cushioning and restraints: it sounds so sexual. Of course, every single thing a man says, I remind myself, will sound sexual. Everything has sounded sexual since I had sex for the first time. The world unveiled, reconfigured, divided between those with boy parts and those with girl parts.

He's waiting for my response, so I try. "I'm just trying to think what my mother would say. She's not speaking to me since I'm dropping out of school, but she'd know what I needed. She'd know if the furniture pads are necessary or a rip-off."

"Hey, look, if it was me, I'd go with a few pads. They're cheap—heck, for you, they're free—and I think the straps aren't necessary. But the insurance, the insurance is not a bad idea. All that way—it's a long drive, and no one plans an accident."

I take his advice, pay, and slide the key with its U-Haul keychain onto my empty BU key ring. I start towards my truck, these keys an unaccustomed weight in my palm.

YOUR FIVE FAILED JOBS

by Kevin Wilson

I.   ADOLESCENCE (THE FIRST JOB)

A. You clean a three-story building where insurance is sold. You come in ten minutes after the regular office workers have left for the day. You think your father helped you get this job but you might have just filled out an application. You hate mopping; you love dusting. Vacuuming you can take or leave.

B. You read so many comic books in that building. You jerk off to so many comic books in that building. You always clean up after yourself.

C. You keep putting paper towels in the toilet, which, apparently, damages the pipes. Even though you are warned on three separate occasions, by a man who has to stay at work ten minutes later than he needs to, you keep doing it. You are so relieved when he does not tell you that there are office security cameras in the building and they have recorded the countless times you have jerked off to comic books that you instantly forget his actual warning. Is there any need to continue this part of the story? You break the toilets.

D. It is an easy enough job to leave; you simply do not show up that night and there is no one around to take note of this. Your mother catches you jerking off to comic books in the closet of your room and makes you bury them in the yard, each issue, wrapped in plastic, backed with cardboard, under the earth.

II. COLLEGE (IN BETWEEN CLASSES)

A. You don't wear a suit to the interview. The only suit you own is for funerals and so you just wear a short sleeve button up and a black tie (your funeral tie). Your future boss asks if you are familiar with HTML. You have heard of this, vaguely, yes. You nod your head. You expect him to continue, to then elaborate on HTML, to expand your admittedly limited knowledge of these four letters. You are hoping he will tell you what HTML stands for. Perhaps he will even turn his computer screen towards you and show you a demonstration of HTML. He does none of these things. He simply says, "Well, if you're familiar with HTML, then you'll do fine." You have the job. You cannot give it back.

B. Your office is the size of a closet and you scan a policy and procedure manual into the computer and then convert it to HTML. The day after your interview, you buy a book called *HTML For Dummies* and you keep it next to the unscanned pages of the manual. No one ever comes to check on your progress. You are a student worker and they are unsure of your hours.

C.   You have never used the internet before. It is newish in general and entirely new to you. You search your name on a search engine and nothing comes back. Your interest in the internet wanes. Someone at the university, a professor or a doctor or perhaps just a director of admissions, is fired for downloading pictures of women dressed up like cats from the internet on his office computer. Your interest in the internet returns.

D.   You jerk off to some random naked woman on the internet in your closet of an office and your boss walks in on you. He walks right back out. Two days later, your desk and computer and the 875-page manual are moved into the boss's office. Your back is to him, your screen visible. He never discusses this with you, never reprimands you. You have no idea where to place *HTML For Dummies* to avoid its detection so you leave it at home and just make do without it.

E.   You graduate at the exact same time that you finish putting the policy and procedures manual on the internet. It is almost like you planned it, though you did not. You have changed the text in some sections. You have inserted your name in several places. In a section on "Publishing and Printing in the University," you add the phrase THE EDGE IS A SHANTY TOWN FILLED WITH GOLD-SEEKERS. WE ARE THE NEW FUGITIVES AND THE LAW IS SKINNY WITH HUNGER FOR US in a paragraph on copyright issues.

It is never detected and, from time to time, you check the website to make sure it has not been amended. It never has.

III. ON YOUR OWN (YOUNG AND UPWARDLY MOBILE)

A.   Your girlfriend is going to be a doctor. She is going to a prestigious medical school in the Northeast. You decide to follow her at the last second, quitting a job at a dairy farm that lasted seven days, living in a trailer, cow shit everywhere. You, inexplicably, get a job as an assistant to an incredibly well known and influential author who directs the women's studies program at the very same prestigious school in the Northeast that your girlfriend now attends. You minored in women's studies in college, which human resources loves. You decide not to tell them that, actually, the women's studies program was lacking at your small, southern university and the classes consisted of reading little known works by women authors. You have never read a single book by the famous author in any of your women's studies classes. Not even an article. You meet with the author, who is incredibly beautiful and finds your accent charming. You get the goddamn job.

B.   A doctoral student, when you refuse to make copies for him on the weekend, calls you a fucking hick in an email. You walk twenty minutes in the snow, still too stupid to buy a winter coat, to the office copy room, where the doctoral student is having to make his own copies for a conference later that week, and call him a fucking cocksucker. You think perhaps a fight is going to occur, but instead he stares at you, mouth wide open. You cannot think of how to proceed, how to extricate yourself from the situation, and so you help him make copies for the rest of the afternoon in complete and total silence. At the university disciplinary hearing, he loses his stipend and you are not fired or reprimanded because you have printed off his email and no one believes that you would walk twenty minutes in the snow, call him a fucking cocksucker, and then help him make copies for the rest of the afternoon. The famous author, who hates doctoral students, finds all of this charming.

C.   Your girlfriend, now dissecting bodies and not sleeping (not having sex with you and also simply not closing her eyes at night and resting for six to eight hours), breaks up with you. You make a pass at the famous author and she reciprocates and you fuck in the bathroom at a gallery opening. She starts calling you her protégé. Your ex-girlfriend will not return your calls. You start helping the famous author research a book about sex and gender in literature and you spend a lot of time on the phone, making international calls to publishing companies in Europe for reprint permissions. You start sleeping at the office so the famous author can tell her husband that she is going to the office to get work done at night.

D.   The famous author gets a one-year position at an even

more prestigious university in the Northeast. You cannot go with her or it will look suspicious, though everyone in the department already knows. You start bringing six packs of beer to work and hiding the empties in your desk. People think you are broken up about the famous author and 9/11, but really you are just so fucking cold and how do people live here for their entire lives? You call the famous author every day, to read her mail to her, but instead of typing out her replies and mailing them out, you throw all the correspondence in the trash. You start drinking a whiskey made in Tennessee, which you never drank when you were in the South (not the famous whiskey but the other one). You pass out in the elevator at work one night and when you wake up you are in a hospital. You wonder if you are fired but someone finally tells you that you are on medical leave.

E.   Your parents come visit you and have you moved to a very prestigious psychiatric ward in the Northeast, though your father keeps saying, "It costs as much as college." You get to wear street clothes in the ward, which both amazes and irritates you. You start getting better and then you find out that the women's studies program has been discontinued because the famous author has decided to accept a full-time position at the more prestigious university in the Northeast. You keep thinking, irrationally, that your ex-girlfriend, though she is only a little less than two years into medical school, will be doing rounds in the ward, but of course she isn't.

F.   When your stay at the ward has ended, your parents drive all the way to check you out and then drive you all the way back home. You never officially quit your job or get fired, but you are certain that they are aware of your intentions. You live with your parents for six weeks, wearing the same blue sweater every day, helping your mother make meals that you see on the Food Network. Your father tells you to leave the decision making up to him, that he will find you a good job, and you decide to let someone else take over for a while. Late one night, with a flashlight and a garden shovel, you dig up your old comics. They are surprisingly well preserved. You jerk off behind the stacked cords of wood, staring at the winged feet of the Sub-Mariner. You wish you could stay at home forever.

IV. THE SECOND TRY (BACK IN THE WORLD)

A.   Your father gets you a job at the local newspaper, where you serve as the assistant to the head sportswriter. You rent a small apartment above the now-closed hardware store in the town square, which means you can walk to work. The head sportswriter wears a fedora and carries a pocket watch and has two cameras that he takes to local events, one for the paper and a strange, plastic, Russian camera that he uses to take pictures of attractive women in the stands, on the street, on the basketball court. You steal some of these photos and take them back to your apartment and jerk off to them, the strange, heightened colors and tricks of light, the way the thing is and isn't what it appears to be.

B.   You develop a crush on the coach of the female cross-country team at the high school that you once attended. She is pale and freckled and blond and tiny and so ethereal that you would not be surprised if her feet did not touch the ground while she ran. And she does run. She runs with her team, always at the front, pacing them, then outrunning them, then waiting for them at the finish, lying on her back in the grass. You ask the head sportswriter for a camera so you can add depth to the pieces that you supply to him, for his headline. He refuses, is the one who carries the cameras, and so you steal the few pictures he has of the cross-country coach, two or three photos because she doesn't, as he says, really do it for me.

C.   The coach of the female cross-country team runs toward you and you, hanging over the chain-link fence, do not think to run away. "What do you think you're doing here every day?" she asks you. "You are making my runners slow." You are smart enough to say that you are writing a story for the newspaper, flash your credentials, a laminated business card with the address of the paper. "Well," she says, running back to her team, "effing write it already." She does not say fucking, she says effing. You are going to steal that Russian camera tonight.

D.   You decide that you better actually write a story about the cross-country team. The coach is unapproachable at this point, still so effing irritated with you. The girls are now in danger of losing the regional finals. You talk to the runners and they say the coach is very good, very motivating. You ask them if she is seeing anyone. One of the runners, who tells you she is going to keep running until she gets a scholarship and then when she finishes college, she's going to eat food that she likes, says that the coach is not seeing anyone. "She's asked about you," she says, and you smile. "Were you really in a mental institution?" she asks. You nod, hope your honesty will get back to the coach and she will appreciate this.

E. "You stole my fucking camera," the head sportswriter says to you. You do not answer. The story about the cross-country team runs with your byline because cross-country does not, as the head sportswriter often says, really do it for me. You leave work early to bring the paper to the cross-country coach and the girls start smiling when you arrive, have already seen the article apparently. The coach walks over to you, slowly, her head down. "That was a very good article," she says. You ask her to dinner and she says yes.

F. Without evidence, though still certain that you stole the camera, the head sportswriter informs you that you have been fired. "You left work early yesterday," he says, enjoying himself, "without permission." You want to tell him that you have jerked off at work, fucked your boss, gotten drunk and passed out in the elevator and you were never fired. Instead, you pack up your things and leave, hoping your parents will not force you to go back to the psychiatric ward in the Northeast. At dinner, your third date with the cross-country coach, the topic of your firing never comes up, doesn't seem important. You will, you tell yourself, find something better, or at least just as good, or perhaps even worse, but something you can do.

V.   THE REAL JOB (ALL GROWN UP)

A.   The cross-country coach guides the team to a state championship and, in the summer, she accepts a position at a private girls' school on the other side of the mountain, where she will only have to coach cross-country and won't have to teach civics or Tennessee history or a state-edited and dangerously misinformed sex ed class. She wants you to go with her. You want to marry her, but she, for now, just wants you to go with her. You, without a stick of furniture, having never made anything work correctly for longer than a few months, agree.

B.   You get a job at the same private girls' school, which does not require state certification and is happy to have you. You teach little-known works by women authors, books that are crazier and more interesting than you first realized, to high school juniors. The cross-country coach takes the team from dead last to the state championship and does not seem to think this is a big deal. You wish you could write a story about it for the local newspaper. Instead, you are writing a novel, large and cumbersome and certain to be a failure, but you keep writing it, content

86

to simply work your way to the end of something without exploding, without making a mess to walk away from.

C. You have not failed yet. You have gone a long time without doing something that you have to shake your head repeatedly and hum to forget about. You know the failure will come, that it is inevitable, but you are so happy, almost insanely so, to have done so well, that when the failure comes, when you accidentally kiss a student or call the head of the English Department a limp dick motherfucker, you will be ready, will accept your punishment and step into what is next, the new thing that you have made with your own two hands.

SHELTER BY
SHENA
MCAULIFFE

SHELTER

by Shena McAuliffe

PHOTOGRAPHS, 1975

Hand in hand on the steps of a clapboard church, Patrick and Catherine smile. She wears an A-line dress of white cotton, pearl buttons up the back, a blue sash at the waist. On her head, a wide-brimmed hat, a length of ribbon flips in the wind. Her dark hair gleams and behind her back, Patrick tugs a greedy handful. He wears a navy suit with a polka-dot bow tie. He has long sideburns and bad teeth: cavities, football accidents, and a flight over the handlebars. Gold glints in his smile. Both are thin, and he is tall.

As the camera shutter closes and the flash explodes, Catherine's hat catches the wind and soars. Patrick laughs, so many teeth, and Catherine reaches for her hat. The other hand is on her head. Her mouth, too, is open, but wider, shrieking.

The second photo is perfect.

SPLINTER

First there is Daisy, a gray cat, with long, soft fur. By night she hunts the fields around their windblown farmhouse. She eats her prey at the foot of their bed. Half asleep, they hear the crunching of little bones, the rhythm of a careful tongue cleaning up after a meal. In the morning they can tell: this was a rabbit—this slick dark liver. This a bird—this little clawed foot. Or a mouse—these tiny vertebrae.

One afternoon Daisy brings a live rabbit into the kitchen and drops it, proudly, at Catherine's feet. It's a harmless, quivering thing, but Catherine is unsettled by its heaving sides, its flashing eyes. She considers calling Patrick at the shipyard and looks out the window at the yellow cornfield. It's almost winter; a rabbit is a small thing. Beneath the sink she finds a pair of rubber gloves and pulls them on. She kneels and nudges the rabbit into a paper sack, which she holds at arm's length as she carries it to the edge of the cornfield. She sets it down like a flower on a grave. With her toe, she tips the bag on its side, but the rabbit doesn't come out.

A year later, a month after their first anniversary, when Catherine is pregnant, they move to a house on a dead end road, beside a lily pond littered with sunken rowboats and home to a pair of sandhill cranes. It is quiet, hidden from wind and traffic. Patrick affixes their name to the battered mailbox and builds a split rail fence along the property line. They pour concrete for a brick patio and mark the corners with iron stakes.

It is still dark the morning Daisy jumps from the second story balcony and lands on a stake. Patrick and Catherine are startled awake by her howls. Catherine watches from the deck while Patrick goes to her. He is afraid to lift her, afraid of causing more damage. He tries to touch her head but she tenses and snaps. Catherine calls the vet, who takes the cat, stake and all, to the clinic. As if they had shrunk from the invader, Daisy's vital organs are unharmed, but she never fully recovers. She develops oozing abscesses. She stumbles.

THE LUNCHBOX

Every weekday morning Patrick carries his aluminum lunchbox across the parking lot at work. At 7:30 a siren sounds, signaling the shift change, and the night workers stumble from the doors, shaking their limbs and rubbing their eyes in the daylight. One morning, as the workers are weaving between each other, Patrick bumps a man with his lunchbox, and, tired and grumpy, the man shoves him. Patrick collides with the man's friend and a fight breaks out. Patrick swings his lunchbox into someone's skull, and the lunchbox springs open: a hardboiled egg. A foil-wrapped sandwich. A thermos. A paper napkin, neatly folded. The men are restrained. Patrick is suspended from work for three days.

"You could've killed someone," his supervisor says.

Patrick says, "I didn't hit him that hard."

Catherine packs his lunches in brown paper bags.

SENTINELS

There are two children: Margaret, who they call Maggie, and Nora, born twenty months apart. After Nora is born, Patrick plants a blue spruce for each of his daughters, one on either side of the front door, far enough from the house that their branches and roots can extend without touching it.

Maggie is self-assured and tough, with a tangled cap of curls, not quite blond, and quick, sturdy legs. She speaks in staccato syllables. "I'd like a ham-bur-ger," she says. "Yes. Please. I would like ketch-up." She practices throwing a foam football until the spiral is tight, there is no wobble. The first time it spins smoothly, she rushes to pick it up, and spikes it in the grass. Maggie's face is always smudged: mud on her earlobe, dandelion yellow beneath her chin.

Nora is quiet with dark hair and small eyes. She watches Daisy pick her way through brightly colored wooden blocks on her way to a patch of sun. She does not point. When Catherine zooms a spoonful of pureed carrots into her mouth she opens wide, blinks, and does not laugh. No carrots ooze at the corners of her lips. Patrick grips her foot, which dangles from the highchair, between his fingers and pulls her sock until Nora kicks, and the sock slips off.

"I've got your sock," Patrick says, waving the sock, and Nora studies him, tips her head slightly, opens her mouth for more carrots.

When Nora learns to walk, she often runs in circles until she falls.

RELIABLE

On summer nights, when Nora is almost three, Catherine buckles her into a plastic seat on the back of her bike and they ride along the cedar drive, away from their lily pond, past their beat-up mailbox, through the darkness to Lake Michigan. The bike tires bump over tar-patched cracks, and they watch the silver-black ribbon of water unfurl before them.

"Faster," says Nora. She hums one low note, holds it. "Look. The moon is following us."

"Mmm-hmm."

"Let's walk to it—like Jesus of Nazareth."

Back home, Nora finds a window from which she can wave goodnight to the moon. By the next week, she has to run down the driveway to see it hovering above the trees, and she waves like a pageant queen. On the night of the new moon Nora sulks, twists in the bed sheets.

Catherine sits on the edge of the bed and Patrick stands in the doorway with a flashlight. "Look here, Nor," he says, and raises the flashlight to his mouth, stretches his lips around it and switches it on. His cheeks glow red, taut and fibrous. He pulls the light out of his mouth to say, "I'm the man in the moon," and then puts it back and opens his eyes wide. Nora shrieks.

"Jesus, Patrick. You're scaring me," says Catherine, turning on the bedside lamp. "Sweetie," she says to Nora, smoothing her hair. "There are things we can't control in life, and the moon is one of them. It'll be back."

"When?"

"Soon—tomorrow. Or the next night."

"How do you know?"

"It's one of those things you can count on," Patrick says from the doorway.

"Like a best friend?"

"Well, sort of. The moon's just a rock," says Catherine. "A cold, dusty rock. It doesn't have feelings."

"A big rock," says Patrick. "The biggest."

"It glows because the sun shines on it." Catherine leans towards the lamp and her face glows brighter. "Like this. Think of this lamp as the sun."

Nora starts to cry and Catherine tucks her thin hair behind her ear, tries to pull her close, but she pushes her mother away. She seals herself under her quilt. Catherine sits on the edge of the bed until Nora kicks her blankets aside, plucks a shoe from the floor, and flings it at the wall.

WEEDS

When the snow melts, Catherine and the girls pull fistfuls of last year's weeds from a ten-by-ten foot garden plot. They plants peas, cabbage, carrots. They build four bamboo teepees for tomatoes and beans, but by July the garden is overtaken by white-flowering garlic mustard. Catherine spends hours weeding; the carrot greens grow spindly and pale. The mustard wraps around the bean teepees, holds tight.

Nora picks the mustard flowers and bundles them into a bouquet. Catherine snatches it and stuffs it in the burn barrel. Maggie lights the match.

WISH

Standing in the bathroom in striped boxers and socks, leaning into the mirror, Patrick finds a gray hair.

"I'm an old man," he says.

"Oh, please," says Catherine, from the bedroom. "You're a strapping young thing."

"Am I?"

"If you want to look younger you should get your teeth fixed."

He smiles too widely at his reflection. He raises one eyebrow, winks, plucks the gray strand with his thumb and forefinger.

In the bedroom, he offers the hair to Catherine in cupped hands.

"A token of my love," he says.

A puff of breath; she blows it from his hands.

SPY

Maggie, age six, lies on her belly at the edge of the pond, watching the water for tadpoles. Across the water: a movement. The sandhill cranes are as tall as she is, with thin gray necks and black legs hinged with knobby knees. Their beaks are slender and sharp, their heads capped with scarlet feathers.

The smaller crane calls twice, a rattling honk, her beak uptilted. The larger one answers once, pointing his beak to the sky, and they fly, dancing like puppets, legs dangling over the water. The larger one swoops to the bank and pulls loose a tuft of grass. With his beak and a snap of his neck, he flings the grasses and they separate, alight on the surface of the pond.

"Frank," Maggie says, naming the larger bird. "And you'll be Marianne," she says to the smaller one, quietly, across the distance of the pond. The two cranes dance to exhaustion, then land together on the bank.

Once, she watches Frank fight a great blue heron for a stick. Frank loses. The heron flies off, its neck a droopy drainpipe, the stick a black slash across the pale sky. Frank stands in knee deep water, emitting a low, wooden rattle.

She borrows Patrick's binoculars to watch the nest, waiting for the eggs to hatch. She does not invite Nora to look, though sometimes she shares her observations.

"They take turns," she tells Nora one afternoon, untying her muddy shoes in the hallway. "Sometimes Frank sits on the eggs. Sometimes Marianne."

The first egg hatches two days earlier than the second, while Maggie is at school. But she is watching when the second chick hatches, and when the adult cranes leave the nest for food. The older chick repeatedly jabs the new one with its beak. Maggie does not report the death.

CANNIBALS

Every Sunday, at a quarter to ten, Patrick drops Catherine, Maggie, and Nora at the church playground and goes home to read the paper. The girls go to Sunday school while Catherine is in church.

At her First Communion, Maggie wears a wreath of dried baby's breath and a plain dress. She bows her head and accepts the Body of Christ in cupped hands, slips the wafer into her mouth, crosses herself. Her mouth is set in a grim line. She skips the blood; Jesus sticks to the roof of her mouth, papery and dry. She scrapes him off with her tongue, kneels and bows her head, but her eyes are flashing, wide, still looking up: boys with ties cinched at their throats. Girls in sheer veils. Hunched old women, their knotted hands curled loosely at their sides. Men in slim suits, a carnation in a button hole, a handkerchief in a pocket. Men in boots.

After church, Patrick drives them to a restaurant and the girls order waffles with strawberries and whipped cream.

"Isn't it like being a cannibal?" Maggie asks.

"Don't talk with your mouth full," says Patrick. Maggie swallows.

"But isn't it?"

"It's complicated," Catherine says. She reaches across the table and wipes Nora's chin.

"Think of it as a symbol," says Patrick.

"But Sister Theodora says it's really Him after the priest blesses it."

"Well, does it taste like a human body?" asks Patrick.

"It tastes like paper."

"Well, then...."

Maggie sets her fork down, looks Patrick in the eye. "How would I know what a body tastes like, Dad?"

"You've eaten meat."

"Gross."

"Yeah gross," says Nora.

"Why don't you go to church with us?" Maggie asks.

"Why don't I go to church? I don't go to church because I don't believe in God."

"Patrick," says Catherine.

"She asked. You want me to lie?"

"I don't believe in God either," says Nora, her mouth full of waffles.

NIGHTCAP

Patrick likes his whisky straight. Catherine likes a gimlet—gin. The children are sleeping. Patrick and Catherine sit on the patio in the dark, his feet in her lap. They pick green olives from a jar. Patrick licks the salt from Catherine's lips, throws his head back, calls to her like the cranes. She laughs and pushes an olive into his mouth and he chokes. He spits the olive into his hand.

STRAY

It is the morning of her first day of second grade. Maggie, wearing shorts and tube socks, is dragging a trashcan to the end of the driveway. She sees a glint of orange; a hunter's arrow stuck in the side of the garage. She squints into the trees, sees nothing. She pulls the arrow out by the shaft, but the tip stays buried in the wall. She digs it out with Patrick's screwdriver. It is a streamlined, metal arrowhead, nicked and bent. She reassembles the arrow, fitting the cool black shaft into the tip, smoothing the plastic feathers—two orange, one yellow. She throws it once, like a dart, aiming for a tree trunk. It flies straight, but strikes nothing, arcing quickly to the ground, scattering dirt. She brushes it off. She hides it beneath a stack of folded sweaters in her closet.

SLEEP

Nora laughs in her sleep, so Catherine closes her door at night. In the morning, Daisy waits, sliding her paws beneath the door. During winter, Patrick goes to bed right after dinner, claiming the long hours of darkness make him tired, but he is up each day by four, drinking coffee at the kitchen table. Catherine is a fitful sleeper, often finding herself pushed to the edge of the bed with Patrick's spine pressing into her back, his cold feet touching her legs. Some nights she wakes restless, and goes to the living room and sits in the dark. She listens to the pop and hiss of a record beginning to spin—then the *Cello Suites* or the *Goldberg Variations*. Maggie brushes her teeth each night at 9:15 and closes the door to her room, but often she stays up, flipping through news magazines, cutting out pictures of canyons and jungles and tattooed Maori, Inuit girls in sealskins, men in dance clubs, their faces thick with make-up. She pastes them in a notebook labeled TRAVELS. She builds a tent over her bed with a sheet dyed with beet juice.

MOLT

Cattails blaze like flames around the pond. The cranes are gone for the winter. The grass in front of the house is tall, taller than Nora, taller than Maggie. Nora won't set foot in it, afraid of getting lost, but Maggie plunges through, forming labyrinthine tunnels, tramping a space where she lies and reads for hours.

She catches a pine snake, brown with black diamonds, twisting through the grass. Grasping it below the head, she lifts the tail with her other hand, and holds it high, triumphant, the length stretched between her hands. The tip of its tail curls slowly around her wrist.

"Mom!" Maggie yells, and Catherine appears, framed by the screen door. "Come see!" Catherine pushes the door open. She is drying her hands with a checkered towel.

She laughs. "Well, look at you."

"Can I cook it?" Maggie asks. She's been reading Westerns.

"Cook it?"

"You know—on a fire."

"I don't know, Mags. That sounds messy. And I don't know about snakes. They might have diseases, or bacteria or something. I've never heard of eating one."

"In my books they eat everything," Maggie says. "They eat rattlesnakes."

"Well, ask your father, I guess." Catherine shrugs.

When Patrick gets home from work he agrees, but under the condition that Maggie kill and cut the snake herself.

Maggie carries the snake to the edge of the pond in a plastic bucket, covered with a piece of cardboard. Over her shoulder she carries a spade and a crosscut saw. She spills the snake onto the ground and Patrick steps on it with his boot as it tries to slither away, extending its head, and Maggie strikes it with the spade. She pauses after the first blow, although the snake is still alive. It pulls back, trying to coil its head into its body. Maggie has never killed anything larger than a fish. She strikes it again, twice, and it stops moving. She saws its head off while Patrick goes inside to wash his hands, although he has not touched anything.

By the time Patrick returns she has sliced along the snake's belly, and is removing the skin with deft tugs. Patrick gathers deadwood. Maggie cooks chunks of meat on a skewer over a fire and the smell is slightly sweet. It cooks quickly, blackening without sizzle or pop.

Seated at the picnic table, Maggie offers her plate to Nora, who takes a delicate bite and chews carefully, before pushing it back to Maggie, who laughs and finishes the rest.

"Next, I want to try possum," Maggie says.

Catherine shakes her head. "Whose kid are you?"

SCOLDS

A pie on the counter, crust nibbled away. Maggie's new blue jeans in the hamper with a torn knee. A dead bird, wrapped neatly in tissue, stashed in Nora's patent leather shoe. Over and over, the screen door snaps on its hinges, bangs closed. A penguin drawn on the steamed window of the Buick shows up ghostly every time the windows fog. A tin of tobacco nests in Patrick's jacket pocket. Water boils away on the stove, gray smoke, a burned-black pot. Maggie misses the bus, walks home from school singing, alone. Nora watches *Jaws* on late-night TV; nightmares give her away. A missed pill; a missed period. Sour milk pushed to the back of the fridge, curdles running down the drain. A miscarriage; Catherine curls in a dark room, her secret spoiled.

PERCUSSION

At dinner Nora clinks her fork against her glass.

"Kiss. Kiss," she orders her parents.

Catherine takes the fork away, says, "Eat your potatoes."

ROLLER PINK

In Patrick and Catherine's bedroom a door leads to the unfinished loft, full of boxes and wrapping paper, window fans, an old bicycle, an American flag—neatly folded. The walls are naked insulation, pink fiberglass, which Maggie and Nora learn not to touch, but not until Nora has developed a rash up the back of one leg. The floors are yellow particleboard, and the room seems to glow and hold its breath. The girls bring their father's shop radio from the garage and push the boxes against one wall. They circle the new space in their rollerskates.

"Reverse skate!" Maggie announces, and they switch direction.

They set up a limbo game with a yardstick and boxes, but find it is too difficult to lower the stick, almost impossible to find and position enough evenly-sized boxes while wearing skates. They give up.

At the back of the loft, there is a pair of doors that, when opened, look onto the lily pond. If the loft were finished, these doors would exit to a balcony or stairway, but as it is, they open into hazy, green air, dust suspended in sunlight, occasional blowing leaves. The girls are forbidden to open these doors, but when they know their mother is in the kitchen, their father is at work, they swing the doors open and sit in the doorway, skates dangling. They throw things: loose nails, chewing gum, an apple core.

LOOKER

Catherine is planting irises around the mailbox while Nora and Maggie play Go Fish in the grass. She wears a sun hat and a bright pink bathing suit, her bare shoulders tanned and freckled. From a passing car, a whistle.

"Whoo, Mom," says Maggie. "Maybe you better put on a shirt."

"Why should I?" Catherine says.

"You're a married woman," says Maggie.

"So? It's nice to get some attention once in a while."

"Shouldn't you get your attention from Dad?" says Nora. Catherine packs the dirt tight around a bulb and straightens.

"Well, I do, but married women like to know they've still got what it takes." She smiles and wipes the sweat from her temple with the back of her hand.

RESIDUE

Patrick's sweat smells like raisins. Shaking out his t-shirts in the laundry room, Catherine smells it—sleepy, rich, a little sour. The smell is in the bed sheets. And in his shoes, right after he takes them off.

"Raisins," she says, when he is undressing at night, and he throws his t-shirt at her. She throws it back, says, "If you ever die, the sight of oatmeal on the stove will make me cry."

He lies down and she bites his shoulder. She bites her own lip, hard, draws blood. Patrick pulls her close.

COMET

The winter the comet is in the sky, Patrick says, "Once every seventy-six years, girls. A once in a lifetime chance, girls. Next time it's visible, you'll be old women. Blind, probably. And I'll be dead."

He takes the girls to a beach early in the morning. Six inches of crusty snow push up Nora's pants and scrape her skin. Patrick stands between his daughters, binoculars raised to the black sky. He knows from his star charts where the comet should be, but he cannot find it. The girls each take a turn with the binoculars, but see only bright jumbled stars, black. Even snug in their boots, their toes begin to hurt, then tingle and buzz. Along the surface of the lake, the sky grows blue and they walk to the car.

Two weeks later, Patrick is sitting in the backyard, drinking beer from a bottle, when he sees it. He calls them, but Catherine is washing dishes. The girls shiver in nightgowns and boots.

"That's it?" says Maggie, following Patrick's finger. "That?"

"Mom!" Nora calls. "Come out."

The three stand, watching the sky. Finally, they hear the door open behind them and Catherine joins them.

"So you found it," she says. Patrick hooks an arm loosely around her neck.

"So we found it," he says.

"Is it all it's cracked up to be?" Catherine says, squinting.

"Yes," says Nora.

"No," say Patrick and Maggie.

"What did you expect?" Nora says. No one answers. Nora blows the comet a kiss. "You're splendid, darling," she says. "Grand." To her family she says, "It's old, that comet."

The comet looks like an icy thumbprint—a tiny, dusty smudge.

SURPRISE

Maggie hides behind the bathroom door, feeling her heart beat in her throat. She makes certain her toes are not peeking, her shadow is not stretched across the wall. Her shoulder blades press against the wall. She tries to silence her breathing. Patrick's boots clomp in the hallway. She waits, watched his silhouette beneath the door. His hand is on the doorknob.

Maggie jumps out, shouts, "Ha!"

Patrick grabs her forearm.

"Don't ever. Do that. Again."

Later, Patrick knocks on Maggie's door. She doesn't answer. He knocks again, pushes the door open, slowly.

"Hey," he says. "I'm sorry." She doesn't look at him.

At dinner he makes a new rule: no jumping out, no surprises.

PORTRAITS

In her second grade school picture, Maggie wears the faux beavertail hat Patrick bought her at Frontierland. At first, Catherine refuses to hang the portrait in the hall, next to

Nora's kindergarten picture. In her third grade picture, Maggie is missing three teeth, and laughs with an open mouth. In fourth grade, a half hour before the class lines up for individual photos, Maggie excuses herself to the bathroom, where she cuts off her shoulder-length curls with plastic-handled scissors. She leaves her hair in the sink. In the fifth grade, she wears a fuzzy pink sweater and pink lipstick. She stuffs her training bra. She cocks her head slightly to the side, smiles with half her mouth, flutters her eyelids lazily.

CINEMA

Catherine closes her eyes and leans back on the sofa. A cello trills and sustains. Nora, barefoot, stands in the doorway.

"Mom," Nora whispers. "Mom, what are you doing?"

"You're up early," Catherine says, straightening up. "I'm listening to a record."

"Are you sad?" Nora asks.

"No. I'm not sad. Come here." Catherine pats the cushion next to her and Nora crosses the room and sits down. "Close your eyes. I like to make up a movie that only I can see. A movie that goes with the music." Catherine closes her eyes. Nora watches.

"What's happening?" Nora asks.

After a minute Catherine answers. "An ice skater with a long scarf. It's snowing a little and she is going somewhere, skating across a lake. I can see her breath."

Nora closes her eyes.

CHERNOBYL

Televised voices twist up the stairs to Nora, lying on her back in the dark, and to Maggie, huddled with a flashlight and a magazine. For hours, the voices drone on, their low cant broken only by the electronic blips and scales of news music. At breakfast, Catherine's hair is ragged and uncombed. Maggie and Nora usually take the bus to school, but today, Catherine drives them.

When she picks them up, Nora sits in back. Maggie throws her backpack in first, sits shotgun, rolls down the window. She puts a hand out into the bold sun.

"Dirk Nelson says a poison cloud is coming from Russia. He says it will kill us, or make us grow an extra head," she says.

"Roll your window up, please," Catherine says. "It isn't that warm."

Maggie pulls her hand in, but leaves the window down. "Dirk said he saw it on the news—that the president said so."

Catherine covers her face with one hand, rubs her eyes, exhales. "Dirk Nelson's wrong."

"But the president said."

"There was an accident in Russia, an explosion," says Catherine. "No one knows what will happen, but Russia is far, far away from here. You won't grow an extra head."

"But we could die?"

"You won't die."

"How do you know?"

"It's very far away. The cloud will fall apart before it gets here. People did die, though. People there died."

"Babies?" asks Nora.

"Yes, babies. Babies. Mothers. Fathers. Everyone."

"But——."

"I don't want to talk about this."

"Can I watch the news?" asks Maggie.

"No. Roll up your window."

SMOOTH

In the shower, Maggie cuts her shin with Catherine's razor. The cut grows white, then bleeds, five inches long. Blood braids with water; Maggie turns the shower off. She tamps the cut with toilet paper, but when she pulls the paper off, the wound reopens. She fills the trashcan, crumples clean tissues on top. She sticks band-aids horizontally across the cut, eight of them, and ties a bandanna tight around her leg. She wears sweatpants, rinses the razor, sets it in her parents' shower, behind the bottle of shampoo. The uncut leg she shows to Nora, sliding her pants leg up to her knee.

"You look like a plucked chicken," Nora says.

"Well, plucked chickens are sexier than feathery ones," Maggie says.

DROWNER

Nora draws on the front step with a chunk of sandstone: A jack-o-lantern. A brontosaurus with leaves hanging from its mouth. She writes GIRAFFE, and draws one, with excessively knobby knees. A candle with a tear-shaped flame and a halo. A many-windowed building burning. A girl in a skirt, beneath jagged waves, bubbles in a vertical line from her open mouth. She draws a thought cloud, fills it with the word FUCK.

She is sent to her room without dinner. All weekend she rakes leaves into piles. Maggie jumps in them. Nora rakes again. She washes dishes, cleans the refrigerator.

The yellow sandstone washes away, but pale scratches remain.

PURE

Catherine is out grocery shopping when the salesman makes his way up the walk and between the sentinel spruces, now ten feet tall. Maggie answers the door, but leaves the screen latched.

"Your mother home, little lady?" the salesman asks. He wears a brown felt hat and loafers with fringe. His face is ruddy and slightly pocked, but his nose is straight and his brown eyes clear and wide-set.

"Nope."

"How 'bout your father?"

"Nope."

"You have a grandma hiding in there?" He leans in, looking over Maggie's head, into the house.

"No," Maggie says, standing straighter.

"Well, can I leave these with you?" The man fans out an assortment of brochures.

"No."

"They're about drinking water. You just can't over-purify your water these days. I'll leave them here on the step. You tell your mom they're here," he says, bending to set the brochures down. Maggie opens the screen door into his head. He stumbles back.

"Hey," he says, catching himself. The door snaps shut. Maggie presses her body into the screen and glares.

"Hey," she says.

He walks back down the walk, straightening his hat. He looks over his shoulder and Maggie sticks out her tongue.

INVENTORY

In the trampled grass near the pond, Patrick finds a can of beer, unopened, and a cigar box in a plastic bag: a round pink stone, a Robin Yount baseball card, two wrapped tampons, a cigarette, a Crane's feather, a fork with its stem broken and sharpened, tines bent for gripping, extended at skewed angles.

Maggie is sweeping the garage.

"What is this?" He holds the weapon up, the cigar box

tucked beneath the other arm.

"That's my stuff," Maggie says, reaching for the box, but he shakes the fork at her.

"Where did you get this?"

Maggie narrows her eyes.

"This is a weapon, Maggie." He dumps the contents of the cigar box on the floor and grinds the pile under his boot. "You're grounded."

"I found it," Maggie says. "At school."

"You're still grounded." He backs out of the garage, clutching the fork, his knuckles white.

CRUSH

In the middle of the night, a week before Maggie's twelfth birthday, two high school boys turn onto the dead end road, and pass the beat up mailbox without noticing. They tear along the drive, around the final curve toward the house. In the backseat is a half-empty case of beer, a pair of fishing rods, a flashlight, waders. They drive through a low cluster of junipers, uprooting them, and through the wall of Maggie's bedroom. The house shudders.

The car pushes Maggie's bed into her closet. Maggie sits up screaming. Patrick throws open her bedroom door, stands with his feet planted, his nakedness illuminated by the cockeyed headlights. Plaster and glass are falling, tinkling. The air is hazy with dust, tangy with juniper. He looks across the smoking car, through the torn wall, into the night. He looks at Maggie and picks her up, lifts her from her bed. He carries her from the room where, already, the dust is settling; the dust is falling like snow.

DEPARTURE

Catherine carries Daisy to the far side of the pond. The cat is too light; Catherine feels her knobby ribs through her fur. She sets her at the edge of the knee-high grass. She runs a finger along the cat's throat, scratches her threadbare ears, slides her hand over Daisy's boney hips, follows her tail to the tip, releases it. Daisy steps into the grass. Lopsided, she picks her way through the field.

"A zillion mice," Catherine whispers.

FIRST MARRIAGE

by Kevin Moffett

THEY NOTICED THE odor outside Tucson the day after they got married. They were driving on a bleak stretch of highway and Tad thought they might be near a rendering plant or a dead coyote, but twenty miles later the odor hadn't dissipated. It was putrid and dense and seemed to be getting denser. Amy drove with her hand over her nose while Tad rolled down the windows and breathed.

"Don't worry," he said. "We're not far."

They were headed to Bisbee in a car, a Volvo, that belonged to a man named Gar Floyd who expected them in Jacksonville, Florida, in eight days. This was their destination or, more accurately, their halfway point. The car was part of a program called Drive Way. In Florida they'd be given somebody else's car, which they would drive back to California.

"It's thickening on my tongue," Amy said. "It's like we're being punished."

The odor swelled. It ate at the air. It was as if some giant blood-rancid bird had dragged itself into the back seat and spread its wings and roosted there.

In Bisbee the station attendant sat in the driver's seat and closed his eyes. A few seconds later he stepped out of the car, coughed, wiped his hands on a blue towel, coughed again, and said, "It's animal."

Tad and Amy looked at each other. Amy handed over the keys and she and Tad walked their luggage to their motel: a cluster of Airstream trailers decorated with atomic-print throw pillows and chintz curtains. Theirs was the Royal Manor. Tad rifled through the cabinets while Amy showered. He found an old Saltines tin filled with condoms, a drawer of taped radio shows from the fifties. He found a book with GUEST MEMORIES on the front. He looked through it, the road still humming under him. CACTUS WRENS IN THE OLD CEMETERY. THE SHRINE AT DAWN. ONI MADE HER SPECIAL BEANS!

He found a pen. TODAY'S THE SECOND DAY OF OUR FIRST MARRIAGE, he wrote. WE HAVE NO SPECIAL BEANS, BUT WE'VE TASTED VICTORY AND DEFEAT AND BOTH WERE WONDERFUL.

The last part was something he'd read in a book about the Civil War. It used to be his slogan, when he had a slogan. Now he had no slogan. He listened to Amy mashing shampoo into her hair. He felt consigned and content and resigned. He fished one of the condoms out the tin, undressed, and got under the covers. He felt like a costume waiting to be worn, an odd feeling but not at all disagreeable, not at all.

They climbed a rounded bluff to see the shrine, built by a father to his son. There were plastic carnations and school pictures of a smiling black-haired boy. On the east-facing side of the shrine the pictures had faded to beige in the sun. The shrine seemed cheap, disused. Noticing a shelf for offerings, Tad searched his wallet and found a punch card from the Sub Hut, which he parted with. "Enshrined," he said. He lifted the collar of his shirt and smelled it. It smelled like shirt.

He looked over the town: laundry lines and kiddy pools and satellite dishes mounted to roofs and trained to the same remote object. Farther on, the copper pit, cactus and scrub, barrenness.

He sat down, closed his eyes, and listened to the click-and-advance of Amy's disposable camera. She'd been taking pictures since they left, gathering evidence of their good time. She was sentimental, discreetly. She saved birthday cards. She couldn't pass a missing pet sign without noting how tragic the child's handwriting was. Sometimes when Tad looked at her he saw someone stronger, more permanent and at ease with herself than he would ever be. And other times he saw something less certain, a question unanswered, a teetering pile of wishes....

When he opened his eyes she was scrutinizing the camera. "Won't zoom," she said. The abrupt way she spoke made it sound German. "Hey, maybe they'll take our picture."

A middle-aged couple in khaki shorts and fanny packs approached, their voices seeming to speed up as they neared. The man said, "The clerk at the hotel keeps saying, 'I'd eat the streets. I'd eat the streets.' He's trying to say the streets are clean."

The woman accepted the camera from Amy. She held it to her face and counted, her top lip quivering like a dreaming dog's, three, two, one.

"We got married this morning," Tad said after she returned the camera. "This is our honeymoon."

"How wonderful," the woman said. She surveyed her husband until his truculent expression softened.

"I just realized I left the bouquet in the car," Amy said. She put her hand to her face tentatively. "It's probably ruined."

"We can pick another one," Tad said.

"No. Are you serious?"

He supposed he was. Unthinking, but serious, he supposed. "Of course I'm not serious."

Amy watched him with puzzled amusement. She watched him like a child waiting for a top to spin itself out.

"We're so in love," Tad said to the couple, "we could fall off this bluff and it wouldn't be tragic. It'd be romantic."

"Poetry," the woman said.

"Horseshit," the man mumbled.

There seemed nothing else to say. Tad noticed the couple was dressed identically except for their fanny packs, which were as unalike as could be. This heartened him, the fact that they'd been unable to coordinate the fanny packs.

"Speaking of which," the man said. "I believe one of us stepped in some." They lifted their feet to check. Tad smelled his shirt again, a mixture of fabric and fabric softener. "Don't let Frank ruin your moment," the woman said.

Back in the trailer, Amy lay down and Tad put in a radio show called "No One Left." A man wakes to find that everyone has disappeared. At first the man, who lives alone and despises his neighbors, is thrilled. He goes to the beach, takes what he wants from stores. But soon he's lonely. Six months later he's raving in the streets. "I can't do it anymore!" he says. "I need to be seen!" He goes into a pharmacy and swallows a handful of sleeping pills. Just as he does, a payphone rings, rings again, again.

"What a cruel turn," Amy said.

"It was probably just a telemarketer."

She sighed, exasperated. "You're always saying things like that. Clever, insignificant things."

This seemed excessively bitter, but he let it pass. Besides, she was right. She was almost always right. Recognizing this and conceding to it allowed him a little dignity, he hoped.

She sat up and rubbed lotion onto her shins. She'd packed a battery of lotions to fight the desert air, a lotion for each body part. Tad began kissing her stomach, arms, legs, neck, stopping to smell the different lotions. It was like a theme park, where you could visit eight countries in a single day.

"Are we really married?" she asked.

He held out his hand to show her the thin band of turquoise they'd bought at a souvenir shop near the courthouse.

"I mean, I'm still figuring out how to feel about it. I used to think it'd be like getting my ears pierced. Only, I don't know. More."

"Don't try so hard," he said. "Let's enjoy our honeymoon. We can always get divorced on the way home."

"That's what I mean! You keep doing that, diminishing it. Acting like it's nothing special."

"Finding each other was special, but we've been together three years. Getting married's just confetti after the party."

"We should at least pretend."

Tad felt like he was being led through a series of increasingly smaller doors. "Okay, let's pretend. Let's talk about all the things we'll do."

"Sometimes it's like you're talking underwater." With her thumbnail she scraped at the skin on her knee, then studied the results unfondly. "I mean, I know you're doing your best."

"I always do my best," he said quickly. Then, "What do you mean?"

"I don't know. I'm beat. I'm married."

"Confetti," he said. "Come here."

She acquiesced. Her body was warm, moist, and unsurprising. Tad closed his eyes and pretended they were trapped on a Ferris wheel. It was their first date and they were nervous and then the Ferris wheel stopped. They held hands and soon began kissing and taking off each other's clothes. Tad imagined the Ferris wheel starting up again and spinning faster. Their trailer seemed to buck and sway, in tune with the scenario. Their inhibitions were brittle, they flaked off like skin.

They'd gotten married the day before in Lake Havasu City. Lake Havasu City was HOME OF THE LONDON BRIDGE, the billboards said, but they must have driven past it or across it without realizing it. They parked in front of the courthouse, went inside, and took a number.

Tad, wearing eel-skin boots and a bolo tie, looked like the brother of somebody famous. The judge asked him if he was in the military; it seemed like he was in a hurry, the judge said. The bailiff took pictures with Amy's disposable camera. Afterward he handed her a bag of sample-size dish soaps and detergents, FOR A FRESH HOUSEHOLD, the label said.

She drove while Tad read the owner's manual and reprogrammed the radio stations every hour or so. It felt good to be logging miles, to command something so imperative. They discussed Gar Floyd's likes and dislikes. Gar Floyd liked raggedy women, they decided. Gar Floyd did not like the idea of milking a goat. The rear armrest folded down to reveal an oval opening to the trunk and Tad and Amy tried to guess its purpose before Tad looked it up in the owner's manual. "Snow skis," he told her.

They'd guessed it was where Gar Floyd stowed open beers when the police pulled him over. An air hole in case Gar Floyd was trapped in the trunk.

"Our first marriage," Tad kept saying as they drove south toward Phoenix. They passed cinder-red rocks. Saguaro cactuses shaped like people being robbed. The wildflowers he picked for her bouquet were drying on the dashboard. "What are you thinking about?" he asked her.

"You," she said. "Me. You and me." She was wearing the white linen sundress she'd bought for the ceremony. She looked drugged, lovely. "I'm trying to decide what sort of life we're going to have."

"Uh oh," he said. He reached over to her with an imaginary microphone. "What kind of life are you deciding to have?"

"I can't say really. It's more like a hue, a general mood."

"What kind of mood?"

She peeked down at Tad's hand next to her chin. "Unfamiliar," she said.

Parked between two snoring semis at a highway rest stop, they had sex in the back seat of the Volvo. They planned to do this in every state they crossed. Sex in Gar Floyd's car was a wonderful novelty, like life itself. Back on the highway they passed a Tercel with blinking hazard lights and JUST MARRIED soaped on its back window. Amy honked the horn, Tad waved. Behind the wheel was a bearded man in a tuxedo, and next to him, a woman in a peach-colored dress.

Tad thought, Right here, this moment, no before, no after. He couldn't recall where he'd heard it. It was either from a philosophy book or an aerobics video. He felt a fierce contentment. He wished there was a way to ration it out to make it last longer. But there was no way. It ignited, it burned up, it was gone.

The man in the tuxedo lifted a can of Schlitz and toasted them as they drove past.

The Volvo sat in the garage, a fan perched atop a toolbox blowing into the open door. Tad approached the car and, leaning in, sniffed. The odor reached out like a slap, sharp and undiminished. It smelled to Tad like membrane or groats, not the things but the words.

"At first we thought it was on the engine block," the mechanic said. "It happens, with kitties especially. They crawl up there to get warm. When you start the car, the fan belt just annihilates them. You would've noticed that." He seemed pleased with his story so far. The odor still reached Tad from where he stood, or else it'd stayed in his nose.

"It was a snake, from the looks of it," he continued. "Probably went in through your wheel well and couldn't get out. Starved. We pulled the back seat and there it was. Little old coral snake."

The mechanic paused while the office door creaked open and a black dog trotted out, followed by an elderly man in spotless coveralls. The spotlessness of his uniform seemed proof that he was in charge. The dog lay down the instant he stopped walking. "It's a shame," the man said. "It was a nice car."

"Was?" Tad said, adding, "It's not our car." He looked at his watch. The minute hand pointed to one number, the hour hand to another. "We need to be in Florida in eight days."

The old man laughed noiselessly. "You're just about through with Arizona. All that's left is New Mexico, Texas, a few others. What takes you to Florida?"

"I don't know, what takes you to Florida?"

"I'm asking you. People often have reasons for going to Florida."

"Oh," Tad said. "The way you said it, I thought it was a joke."

The old man laughed again. Just his shoulders shook. "It's no joke, son. It's a goddamn predicament!" The dog perked up when the man raised his voice, and the man patted him softly. "We'll keep air on it, but it takes time. Right now it's a scream. Might be down to a yelp tomorrow. Didn't you say you're on your honeymoon?"

Tad nodded. He was looking into the car at the bouquet, still drying on the dashboard, remembering something before he retrieved it.

"Why are we talking about snakes then? If I were you I'd be celebrating. Hell, I'd be back at your motel having fun. What do you say, Jeff?"

Tad waited for the other mechanic to say something but it turned out that Jeff was the dog. Jeff didn't say anything. "This is ridiculous," Tad said. "Can't you do anything else? This car belongs to a very impatient man."

The old man scratched his shoulder. Where his neck met his clavicle Tad noticed one of those flesh-colored nicotine patches that always made him a little sick to his stomach. "Sure we can," the mechanic said. And then to the other man: "Go in my office and grab that other fan."

Looking at the bouquet once more before he left, Tad left.

He bought a six-pack of beer and walked back to the trailer as the sun set. The horizon was violently radiant and the wind sung with borrowed nostalgia. It was growing colder. He passed the immense copper pit, a fenced-off canyon of wrecked earth at least a half-mile across, staircased and very still. Tad peered through the fence. The damage looked cataclysmic up close, but seen from space it was nothing. Seen from space it didn't amount to a pinprick. This struck him as a nice, comprehensive thing to realize. He wanted to realize more things like it, but it was getting too cold to concentrate. On the road again, he decided that if anybody asked what he was doing he'd say, very casually, "Just passing through." But no one did.

In grade school he used to pretend to chew gum in class. When the teacher asked him to spit it out, he would pretend to swallow it. This was what he remembered while he looked at the bouquet. The old man reminded him of the teacher, something about how he lazily regulated the conversation.

In the trailer, Amy sat on the edge of the bed, her head pitched forward slightly on her long neck, as it did when she was unsure of something. He came closer and she said, "Tad." The word released a smell like sweet dough. "We aren't moving, are we? It feels like we're being pulled behind a truck."

He told her about the snake and waited while his

disappointment became their disappointment. "That's so awful," she said. Tad's impulse was to make her feel better, and why not? There were a hundred ways to make her feel better, a hundred possibilities. But as he stared at the white underside of the comforter, scorched with an iron mark, he was dim with hesitation.

She said, "I was remembering when I was little, how I'd lie naked in bed after a shower. I'd feel this amazing thing happening inside me. This event. Like my body was just the thinnest husk to hide what was going on inside. I'd try to imagine what my husband would be like, what he was doing at that very moment."

"Probably thinking about girls like you, naked in their beds."

"I hope not. I was nine."

"Maybe I was riding my bike. Was it summer?"

"I imagined him traveling a great distance, suffering setbacks."

"A hero, earning his way to you."

She closed her eyes and smiled. Her face looked slightly misshapen. Was something happening inside her? He waited for her face to show signs of relief. He was distracted by the sound of a coyote. Ah-oooooo. So faint and wavering, it sounded like a coyote practicing to be a coyote.

If there was only one way to make Amy feel better, instead of a hundred, he would not have hesitated.

In a few minutes she was asleep, gripping the pillow like

a flotation device, a castaway at rest at sea. The sight of her sleeping always made him a little envious, the way conversations in other languages did. He was ignored, left behind. It seemed unfair that she could close her eyes and make him, sitting right next to her, invisible. As he left the trailer, he made a lot of noise, trying unsuccessfully to wake her.

He carried the beer into the cemetery that neighbored the trailer park. The hundred-year-old tombstones were crooked like tombstones in a Halloween play. KILLED BY INDIANS, some of them said. The ground was loamy and uneven and he suspected he was stepping on unmarked graves so he found a bench and, sipping the beer, watched a distant quiver of spotlights spread out and revolve and reconverge in precise increments, brusquely sweeping the sky.

When he was a child his mother took him to an Indian mound. He was excited for days beforehand but it was just a big green lump scattered with railroad ties. The sort of place you visited without leaving your car. In protest Tad began running up the mound and down, up and down. A man in a blue uniform stopped him and said, "You're running on the bones of my people."

The man's lips held a toothpick. He clenched his jaw, a sheriff ready to pull his gun. He smiled. "Just kidding," he said. "About my people, I mean, not the bones."

Tad thought of a few things he would've said to the man now. His thoughts were a junkyard. He hounded the edges, distracted by any oddity or shiny trinket.

The spotlights danced in the sky as he finished the beer and began constructing a list of demands for himself and Amy. It went: We must take care of each other. We must be the best versions of ourselves. We must inoculate each other from unhappiness.

Contented, feeling as if something serious had been achieved with very little effort, he walked back to the trailer. A pair of tombstones were pitched against each other in an interesting way and Tad scrutinized them like something he might sketch. He felt expansive, blameless, a bit drunk. "Just passing through," he said to the tombstones. He said it how Gar Floyd would. He made it sound dusty.

All night a harsh wind shook the trailer on its moorings and he brought the sound into sleep with him, dreaming that they were being pulled down the highway. Into the unknown, into the unknown. In the morning he was awoken by the ticking of the trailer's metal ceiling in the sun.

They ate breakfast in a diner with framed articles on the wall about paranormal phenomena. They took a tour of the copper mine which was cold and long and garishly informative. Amy sat with the disposable camera in her lap waiting for something photogenic to occur. Their guide, who'd worked in the mine before it closed, said everyone on the train had to ask one question before the tour ended. "Any advice for me and my new wife?" Tad asked him.

He thought about it for a second then said, "Never don't say goodnight."

Afterward they went into antique stores and picked things up and set them down. Amy bought a petrified rock that said OFFICIAL ARIZONA SOUVENIR and a dream catcher for Gar Floyd's rearview mirror. This cheered them for a while. A trifle distresses, a trifle consoles, wasn't that how it went? They looked around for consoling trifles. They returned to the trailer and listened to the radio shows.

A man keeps seeing someone who looks exactly like him. A woman begins speaking another language, one that no one, including her, understands. The shows were really about aloneness, Tad decided. He helped Amy pull off her shirt and then licked a line straight down her back. He licked dots along each side of the line like a surgical scar. He studied her back and tried to decide what else to do.

What else was there to do?

The Volvo had been moved to the front of the service station, one fan blowing into the driver's-side door, another into the rear-passenger door. Beneath the wiper blade was a piece of paper which Tad freed. THE HAPPY HAWKER, it said. WE PAY TOP DOLLARS FOR IMPORTS. There was a drawing of a car with dollar signs for headlights.

He leaned in. The odor, though not as harsh, was still there. Still insistent. The remains of the remains outlived the remains,

Tad thought. And the wildflower bouquet remained on the dashboard. It looked happy there.

Inside the station, the old mechanic sat eating a sandwich half-wrapped in wax paper. He listened to a portable radio and chewed in rhythm, as if eating the song.

"Still stinks," Tad said. "Any more fans?"

He swallowed thoughtfully before speaking. "People used to put dead fish inside hubcaps, as a joke. Maybe someone's playing a joke on you."

"I told you, it's not my car. It's Gar Floyd's."

"Maybe someone's playing a joke on Gar Floyd."

"Maybe. And maybe we're all clowns in a giant circus."

"Maybe."

The other mechanic came in from the garage and whispered something to the old man, who said, "Christ," and stood up with his sandwich. They walked outside. Tad followed them behind the station where, in a packed-dirt clearing, Jeff was stooped over the picked carcass of what looked like a turkey. When he saw the three men, his front shoulders went rigid and he took the carcass's spine in his mouth, waiting, it appeared, for a reason to run away with it.

"He acts like we don't feed him," the younger mechanic said.

The old man breathed through his nose. "He's not acting like anything, Lon. It's instinct. He's made to think every meal's his last. It's how he survives."

"I bet he'd bite me if I tried to snatch it from him."

"What would you do if someone tried to take away your last meal?"

Tad had the feeling that this exchange had occurred before, perhaps hundreds of times. After awhile, Jeff relaxed and began gnawing at the carcass, crunching the bones ostentatiously.

"Stranded in Bisbee," the old man said after awhile, continuing to admire his dog and eat his sandwich. "That could be a hit song. It'd be sad, but not too sad."

"Something's wrong with this place," Tad said. It was one of those things that he didn't know he was going to say until he said it. "We were happy till we got here."

"What rhymes with Bisbee?" the old man said.

"Frisbee," the other mechanic said.

Tad waited for something else to happen. The old man bit so close to the wax paper that Tad was sure he was going to take a hunk out of it, but the old man knew, apparently he knew, what he was doing.

He and Amy had dinner in town. He ordered a buffalo burger because he thought it might make things more exciting but it didn't. The way the waitress handed him the plate and said, "Here's your buffalo," and then later, "How's your buffalo?" and then "How was your buffalo?" depressed him. He felt like a baby with a toy. A man at a nearby table said to the young boy across from him, "Pretty soon, you'll get to sleep in a bulldozer. How's that sound?"

The boy seemed suspicious but interested.

Amy smiled from time to time to let Tad know their mutual silence was okay. The smile was a token that stood for something to say. It reminded him of the edge of a curtain being lifted and let go.

A group of waiters came out of the kitchen singing "Happy Birthday." One of them presented a single-candled cupcake to the boy, set a coffee filter atop his head, and told him to make a wish. The boy kept his eyes shut a very long time, then, all of a sudden, his face came alive again and he blew out the candle.

Tad said, "I keep thinking of that stupid commercial that goes, 'If this hammerhead stops moving, he dies.'" He tossed a napkin over his half-eaten burger. "It's probably not even true."

Amy looked at him solemnly and said, "There is so much we don't know about the hammerhead."

They laughed and then it was quiet again.

"For my birthday one year," she said, "my dad gave me The Odyssey, the children's version. There's a part where Odysseus returns home disguised as a shepherd to claim his wife. His dog is old and blind, but he sniffs him and immediately recognizes him. I loved that part. That's what I always thought my husband would be like."

"Like Odysseus," Tad said.

"No," Amy said. "Like his dog."

They waited for the check. Tad took Amy's hand and kissed it, inhaling the brackish sea-smell of zinc oxide. She brushed crumbs off his shirt. He had a premonition of her doing the same thing fifty years from now, so familiar to each other they'd be strangers. He thought: there is so much and so little we don't know about each other.

Back in the trailer he was restless. More sex? They'd already had sex twice. Doing it again would be strictly remedial; it would diagnose their dissatisfaction. Instead he complained about the trailer, which was starting to seem like a decoration left out too long. The carpet was filthy. The trashcan was filled with condom wrappers and used condoms. Tad threw away an uneaten orange to make the trashcan look more domestic.

Then he had an idea. In his wallet was a Drive Way business card with the phone number of Gar Floyd's motel in Jacksonville. He found the card and dialed the number. After the clerk connected him to Gar Floyd's room, it rang five times before someone on the other end picked up, fumbled the receiver, and said hello.

Amy studied his expression. "Who is it," she whispered.

"Gar Floyd?" Tad asked. Gar Floyd said yes tentatively, as if expecting bad news. He sounded nothing like Gar Floyd.

"You don't know me," Tad said, "but I'm driving your car to Florida. I wanted to tell you that I, that we've, been wondering about you. You spend time in a person's car and you begin to wonder about him."

"Abort," Amy said, waving her hands. "Abort."

Tad had forgotten why he originally wanted to call. Gar Floyd was clearing his throat, breathing roughly. What had he expected Gar Floyd to say? "Oh," he said. "I thought you were calling from the hospital. My wife's getting treatment. She's sick."

"I'm sorry to hear that," Tad said.

"They prescribed these sleeping pills and, ever since, I keep dreaming I'm back in the Air Force. I'm doing something wrong but no one will tell me what. That's just what it was like." He paused to catch his breath. "Listen, my wife's not doing so well. What time is it?"

Tad looked at his watch and told him.

"Well," Gar Floyd said after awhile, "how's the car?"

"It's great," Tad said. "It's a great car."

"The transmission's been rebuilt. The tires are brand new."

"The tires," Tad said, "are unbelievable." He felt his stomach tighten. "We shouldn't have bothered you."

"Who's there with you?"

"Amy, my wife. We're just married." Telling him this, Tad remembered that this was what he'd called to tell him. He thought it would be funny to tell Gar Floyd about getting married. "We're in Arizona."

Amy stared straight ahead, implacable, like a rigidly disciplined athlete.

"What a great time," Gar Floyd was saying. "Careless."

"Sure," Tad said. "We're seeing all there is to see. Your car's in good hands, that's what I called to tell you. We're checking all the fluids, using high octane. You'll have it in a few days."

"I've got a rental now," Gar Floyd said. "An Escort. It's a

lousy car. The wind blows it all over the road. What kind of car do you drive?"

Tad drove an Escort. He didn't say anything. He watched Amy flop down on the bed and thought about his lousy beef-brown Escort and waited for Gar Floyd to ask another question.

"You woke me up," Gar Floyd said. "The least you can do is talk to me."

Silence on both ends of the line, Tad in Arizona and Gar Floyd in Florida. Tad apologized again. He wished Gar Floyd and his wife well. He stressed the imminence of their arrival. Goodbye, he said. All right, Gar Floyd said.

He sat next to Amy on the bed and patted her arm while she studied the ceiling. "Just married," she said. "Just married. Say it one way and it sounds like one thing. Say it another way and it sounds like something else."

"I thought it'd be funny. It wasn't. What do you want me to say?"

"Nothing, everything. I want you to know when to be serious. Act like this means something."

"I'm excited we're married, I'm ecstatic."

"I'm not just talking about being married."

"What then?"

"This. This moment we're in. Life, Jesus, look at me, you never look at me."

Indeed Tad was staring at the percolator on the counter, at its clear nipple, using it as a focal point. He looked at Amy, at her wide wary face. Whenever she exerted herself her cheeks flushed with ghost acne, like fingerprints on a steamed-up mirror.

She put her hand under his chin and held it strangely. She didn't blink for a long time. "What are you doing?" he asked her.

She let go and said, "Wishing."

After Tad turned off the lamp, passing headlights lurched and danced inside the trailer. He watched them for a few minutes and resolved to leave town in the morning, whether the odor was gone or not. El Paso, Houston, Baton Rouge. He wanted to be looking at Bisbee through a telescope of better days.

"Goodnight," he said.

"Goodnight," she said.

In the morning they walked their luggage to the service station. The Volvo was no longer in front, nor was it inside the garage. Looking around, Tad was surprised by the relief he felt, the sense of absolution.

"Where'd it go?" Amy asked.

Mexico, he hoped, where it'd be stripped, sold, scattered.

"They probably just moved it," he said.

Inside the office, the two mechanics sat next to each other, reading sections of the same newspaper. The younger mechanic looked up and grinned at Tad while the old man kept reading. Jeff was sleeping on a folded towel in the corner, beneath a sign for Bar's Leaks.

"My partner thinks he had an epiphany," the old man said.

"It came to me in a dream," the other man said.

Tad looked at Amy, who had her arms folded over her chest. She knew he was looking at her, he could tell by how her expression went vacant. The four walked behind the station, Jeff trailing behind. The Volvo sat in the clearing with its doors open.

The younger attendant ran to the car, gawkily animated. He arched forward and leaned in for a big cartoon sniff. "Delightful," he said.

"Potpourri," the old man said, shaking his head. "Lime scented."

"Country summer lime," the other mechanic said. "Get in! It smells so damn clean in here!"

Tad and Amy sat in the back seat, their feet crunching down on something as they got in. Tad saw that the floorboards were filled with dark green wood shavings and dried buds. Inhaling the sweet sour smell, he was reminded of those scented soaps he was always tempted to take a bite out of. The dead snake odor was no longer perceptible.

"It isn't bad," Tad said. "It's better than it was."

"My girlfriend buys it in bulk. This is what my bathroom smells like."

The old man sat down in the passenger's seat. Tad hadn't noticed how big he was until he got into the car. He had to slouch forward so his head didn't touch the ceiling. Jeff jumped onto his lap and laid his snout on the headrest, panting.

"No charge," the other mechanic said. "That's the best part."

Tad reached down and grabbed a handful of the rough, ridged wood and then let it go. "No charge," he said to Amy.

"On the road again," she said, holding her hand out for Jeff to sniff, which he did, and then looked around warily. "Will you hand me that?" she said, pointing to the bouquet on the dashboard. The old man groaned as he reached forward and then handed it back to her. It looked brittle, careworn. She held it in her lap.

"No charge!" the young mechanic said. He started the car and pulled out of the clearing, kicking up loose dirt.

Out front, Tad loaded the car. He hung the dream catcher on the rearview mirror while Amy drove off, waving to the mechanics who responded with succinct nods. As they headed east into New Mexico, the landscape started to make sense again and Tad felt an agreeable recession. Time, he knew, was vast—seen from a distance, each moment was nothing, a ripple, barely perceptible, nothing. Soon they would stop at a rest area and make love while other travelers gamboled in their designated areas. They'd stay in a motel shaped like a teepee. By the time they arrived in Florida with Gar Floyd's car, Bisbee would be no more than a minor layover, a place where—look, here's a picture, Amy and Tad smiling at the shrine—they were as happy as they'd ever be.

WILL YOU LOOK
AT THIS

BY

CHRISTINE

SCHUTT

WILL YOU LOOK AT THIS

by Christine Schutt

THE MAN HAS a hole in his foot; it will not heal though he tends it. He flushes the hole with cloudy water; he uses gauze. There's something holy about the way he treats it, his hole, and she does not mean to pun. This is no laughing matter, but his wife walks past quickly. She sees his foot in the cradle of his hands; she only guesses his ministrations, but she knows what's in his bottom drawer. She has seen the orange solutions, the tubes squeezed flat as cans: serious medicine for the serious hole he keeps bandaged.

He wears a golf sock to bed, takes it off in the morning, applies new dressing. When he comes home from work, he tends the hole again. He washes and packs it with gauze. The gauze falls out some nights when he kicks off his golf sock and twitches his wounded foot. He wakes her with his twitching while he sleeps on soundly. In the morning it's she who sleeps soundly straight through to when he is dressed.

"Good morning, sweetheart!"

The showered, fragrant man has a hole in his foot, but doesn't he look handsome! Dressed in a dark suit, his dark puffy shoes don't show and his gait is smooth. He looks happy;

it's the wife who wakes looking flogged. She is all nose and eyebrows, a loose-skinned older woman dewlapped past recognition. "Sleep does nothing for me," the wife says in his athletic leaving, but when the poor man comes home! The wife is modestly improved but he! The man with the hole in his foot is limping. His used suit sighs. "I don't know how much longer I can do this work," he says and hobbles down the hall. He falls back on the made bed and scuffs off his shoes and ticks his leaky foot back and forth very fast. The hole is marked on his stocking, darker and damp.

Is there time before the party to rest? No matter, he does. He sleeps, he lightly snores, and when he wakes, he calls out to his wife, "I'm just going to shower. I'll be out in a minute."

Some minute!

After the shower he goes back to his room and sits naked and props up his foot, spreads a towel on the floor and lays out the tools, a file, a hand mirror, an unguent against neglect. The hole in his foot gets his whole attention. The wife, in passing, once asked, "Have you thought about getting a second opinion?" The man did not respond. The hole in his foot is his secret. He is ashamed of it but also, the wife thinks, a little in love with it.

The wife, seeing the way he holds his foot in his hands, is jealous.

The hole in his foot: is it as big as a quarter or the circumference of a mug? Shallow or cavernous, crusted or soft? She thinks of the other soft parts of him. He has desires still, but exculpatory, preoccupying, ceaseless pain keeps him quiet and still. He says he never travels but by taxi. The man with the hole in his foot says he spends all his money on taxis.

"You should," she says. He stands at work, that's enough— too much really: her thoughts on the matter. At night the dark puffy shoes he wears look thirsty, and the wife is happy when he takes them off and puts them away. The dark puffy shoes are shapeless; they velcro shut. He has a black pair and a brown pair. He has slippers, too, but will not wear them. Why? Why just the golf socks? A stone might sooner answer.

The man with the hole in his foot is cheerful most of the time, but about his damaged foot, he is dour.

"What are you saying? What would you have me do? I'm doing what the doctor said to do."

"What Dr. Bee said to do."

"Yes," he says.

Dr. Bee has examined the man's damaged foot for the past few years, fifteen to be exact, yet it will not heal. Why is that? Oh, she wants to know but she does not ask.

Once she asked, and the man with the hole in his foot pulled his sock off as if it were on fire and yelled at her. He held out his foot so she could see. "Look!" he said, but she didn't, she wouldn't. "Look! Look at this suppurating fucker!"

She said, "I'm only...."

"Only what?"

"Nevermind, nevermind, nevermind, nevermind."

The wife has never met Dr. Bee. Once she said, "As your wife, I have every right to see Dr. Bee." She said this modestly, but the man with the hole in his foot, a man usually inclined to laugh, did not laugh. He did not smile; he simply looked at her sternly and said, "Please," as if he were calling for quiet—and he is. "Please," he says now.

The man with the hole in his foot is still fleet of foot and playful and streaks past her—he has a runner's legs. The hole in his foot is not the consequence of running though it keeps him from running. A sprinter once, like his father before him, he was locally famous. His father died young. The man with the hole in his foot is well past young and so is his wife.

Remember her face on waking? She does. She thinks of her face and more. In the bobsled race toward oblivion come holes and other terms terrible—thinning hair and messy freckles, much too much skin. Also fear. The tick-tock of fear, calm, fear, calm, fear.

"I wish we could stay home," he says and she agrees.

They do not want to go to the party, but they must!

The party is hosted by an efficient client-acquaintance in a spacious frontline top-floor duplex with views of the starry city.

"Welcome, stranger!" Their hostess calls out to the man with the hole in his foot. The hostess has seen him walk in—small steps, no sign of damage—and she is delighted to see him. "My hero," she says. "Do you know what this man has done for me?" the hostess asks the wife who really does know but says she doesn't.

"Your wonderful husband has a new design for the terrace."

Oh, a charmed evening awaits the loved landscape magician.

"How many years have you been at these tricks?"

Everyone knows the answer: "Forever!" He, a showy fish, diaphanously finning through the waters of the city, swimming upward, largely, evermore visible, loved. A beloved man moves through the world largely and lightly, and so he does. The man with the purulent hole in his foot dances his way through the party. Her face is feverish to see him but after the first drink the wife grows dull, duller. What's the matter with her?

She is a character looking down at her reflection in the water. "I know a bank where the wild thyme grows." How often has her husband been puckish with a client: rehearsed at home some handsome Oberon or danced with rude mechanicals and banged around and laughed. She has been lucky—they have been lucky in this buoyant life of theirs together. One more reason he should get his foot fixed. She wants to leave the party this instant!

"Satay?" asks the waiter.

She looks at the waiter as if he has hit her, although she takes up a stick.

"Having fun?" her husband asks.

The pinchbeck specks in his muddy eyes are all she has to

go by for how he feels at the moment. "You?" she asks. "Are you tired? Should we say goodnight?"

"No, no, not just yet, no."

Yes, she is thinking, but only thinking to herself, please, say goodnight to the hostess and her gentle, agile husband; say goodnight to the happy customer who shines at you, asking, "How does it feel to be adored?" The man with the hole in his foot has long been this successful, a loved landscape artist, who makes space where there is none, and brings forth blooms as large as plates.

By comparison, the wife's a barren sullenness. That's how she feels when she sighs in the face of a taxi. After the party, she wants to walk home or halfway at least. It's spring and the street trees are saucy, but there's his foot to consider, and she watches him put out his arm.

Once home, he stays in his dressy clothes watching the game on TV, kneeling on the couch so his feet don't touch though he has kicked off his shoes. He is wearing his fancy suit, his best tie, and he is still in his top coat. He is a man more boy than man, leaning close to the game.

"Oh, your foot must hurt!"

But no, he insists; it doesn't, no; he is fine.

She is the only one in on his secret. Nobody knows what she knows. Dr. Bee doesn't count.

She is afraid of her husband's dying. The skin crumbs she finds, the rusty crusts of his wound in the wells of the bed. "I shake the sheets," she talks to herself. "He's in the air. Help!"

As far as he is concerned, the husband thinks Dr. Bee is all the help he needs; all the help he can get.

Night after night, days, he excuses the pain, saying it's healing, that's all. Again and again, "It's healing," so sincerely uttered; he is a man in visible agony, joking with nurses. The man with the hole in his foot is wholeheartedly good and shames her. But his willful hobble toward oblivion makes her angry! She thinks she might stomp on his foot if he opens their bedroom door, and when he opens the door and discovers what she is doing, she does. She staunches the hole she keeps to herself and presses her foot atop his foot where the shrill skin looks boiled. "Oh! Oh! Oh," on and on! He yelps as much for her as for himself.

"What are you doing?" he demands. What in God's name is she doing? What has she done? "Dear girl!" He is sick with it. "Oh!"—the sight of her wound though she is washing it with a cloth she dips in a cloudy solution—is a horror from which, it seems, he cannot turn away.

"See," she says.

Her wound is the size of a mouth in an "Oh!"

THE GIRLS

by Daniel Wallace

You could always tell the ones he liked the best.

"So, Rachel," he'd ask me, casual as you please. "About how old is she?"

He'd be watching her walk away in the beam of the headlights, after a long and mostly silent ride. For a moment she'd be lit up like a star. She'd turn to wave and my dad would get another look at her ambitious chest, but mostly we had this long look at her butt as she walked down her driveway and paused at her back door, either fishing for a key or waiting for a parent to open it for her. Then she'd wave again, and we'd pull away, going home.

"How old?" he'd ask again.

"My age," I'd invariably say, because how great an age difference are you going to find in ninth grade girls, the pool from which my friends were chosen?

"Fourteen," he said, almost in a whisper.

Fourteen woke my father up. When we were twelve and thirteen he never asked anything about them, only directions to their homes. He'd keep the radio low on a station he liked, and you could hear him listening to it, tuning me and my friends out as he drove his one way once or twice a week.

But when we turned fourteen something happened to him—and to us—that shook him out of his sleep. Until then he had been more of a part-time parent. I mean you could count on Mom for most things all of the time, but Dad—who worked (he sold photocopiers), and when he wasn't working looked to be recovering from it. Dad was there for a certain number of hours a day, usually around dusk during the week, afternoons on the weekends. And there were only certain things you asked him for, things like money and rides and, occasionally, permission. But asking him wasn't usually productive, because he wasn't around enough to know what was permissible, and the things he said were okay sometimes weren't, and I suppose that's why I asked him at all, knowing what Mom's answer would have been all along.

Roused from his sleep, though, he was an inquisitive, clumsy giant. Even so, I don't think anyone would have noticed the change but me; even Mom might not have. It was the situation we were in that made me able to notice, the two of us together in the small space of the car, the routine travel back and forth from our house to the girls'; it was in this very specific circumstance that I was able to see—hard to describe what it was, really. But I saw it, this thing growing inside him like a bud. And I just watched it grow.

"Fourteen," he said again, shaking his head.

"She's mature for her age," I said.

"I'll say," he said. Then, catching himself, glancing at me

sitting still beside him, my face glowing briefly in a street lamp. "She's a very well spoken young lady."

"Whatever."

At a stoplight he tapped his fingers on the steering wheel, eyes roaming through the dark world outside.

"So, did she just move here?"

"Andrea Nichols?" I said. I couldn't believe this. "I've known her since I was in third grade!"

"Andrea? That's Andrea?"

"That's Andrea."

Dad had this thing where in moments of mild surprise he would breathe in deeply through his nose: this is what he did now. In, then out. He was quiet for the rest of the way home, turning things over in his head. It wasn't until we were pulling into the driveway that he spoke again.

"I remember her now," he said.

I took a look at myself in the mirror that night. I had a long one on the back of my bedroom door, and I would close the door and lock it and take off my clothes—all of them, except for my socks—and look at my body. I'd been doing this for the last two years, ever since I came to realize my body's stubborn sameness, its fear of change. I tried to put a space of time between my looks, so something would have a chance to happen, somewhere.

But tonight there was no change at all. Nothing. I don't think I even qualified as having a figure yet, though if I were being optimistic I'd say there were indications of a shape to come. I tried to be positive about it, I really did. But my breasts were like tear drops, and my hips barely rippled at all. Not much there, but then that wasn't the point: the point was who was doing the looking. I simply gazed at what was me and did that thing my father did: breathed in deeply through my nose. Then out.

That summer we started carpooling a lot. Dad would take a load of us to a movie, then someone else would pick us up, or the other way around. Mom stepped in occasionally when it was impossible for him to be there—he did have to work, after all—but he was an eager parent in this regard. He kind of became known as the guy for that. When every other parent failed, there was always my dad, ready and willing to take us wherever we wanted to go. I think I saw him more in the car than I did at home, and if I'm exaggerating it's only by a little.

He liked all of my friends—Andrea, Robin, Ellen, Jennifer— and they liked him back. He had this very well-modulated persona, he knew when to back off, when to laugh, when to ask a question. At home he crawled into his cold fatherly shell, radiating a kind of general dissatisfaction with everything. But riding around with my girl friends he was Mr. Personality. Sometimes I just shook my head in wonder and disgust.

Of course, he about jumped out of his skin when I asked him if he wanted to chaperone a bunch of us girls to the roller skating rink for a party one Friday night. You'd have figured there was no better way for a thirty-nine year old man to spend a Friday night. He didn't scream or dance or anything. But when my father was interested, really interested in something he raised his left eyebrow, just that much; he couldn't help it. And so even though he didn't act excited, I knew when I saw that eyebrow rise he viewed this as the Ultimate Treat.

I thought it sucked. I was through with skating rinks, and now for some reason Robin wanted her party at a skating rink, and I didn't know if I could stand it. Everything at a rink is dirty, and sticky, especially the bathroom door handle, and then these really vulgar boys who come from way out in the county—the same guys who like to hang out at the mall—skate up beside you and try to get your phone number. So yes. I was really looking forward to it.

In the car that night my father smelled like a candy bar.

"Where to, Pumpkin?" he asked, not looking at me but over his shoulder, backing out. I almost didn't answer because of him calling me Pumpkin. It's what he called me when I was a little girl, and I don't think I'd heard the word used that way for a decade. So I gave him a look and breathed in deep.

"Well," I said. "We have to pick up Ellen, Andrea and Jennifer. Robin's going in another car. I'm not sure what the best way is."

"Where's the rink?"

"Durham," I said. "I think. Jennifer has directions."

"Okay. Then I'd say Jennifer first, Ellen second and Andrea third. Sound good?"

"Fine with me."

"Then off we go."

Off we went! At Jennifer's house he honked the horn—once, lightly. I offered to go in after her but he said we could wait a minute: he wanted to see her come out and walk the walk without any possible obstruction from me. His tiny blue eyes peered through the dusty windshield. He had to squint when she finally came. Breathing in and out in short nervous bursts, I thought he might have a heart attack—seriously, it occurred to me. He was that much into it. Jennifer's t-shirts all were about a size too small: her breasts ballooned out of them almost comically. Her hips made a kind of rolling motion when she walked, as if she were dancing. We watched her, my father and I, Jennifer walking toward us in the haze of the orange summer sun. Ellen, the next stop, was a disappointment I'm sure: she was waiting on the curb by her mailbox when we drove up, and slipped in the back seat so quickly he had to turn around in his seat, craning his neck, for a glimpse of taut tanned thigh. She had tight blue shorts on and at the cuff her legs suddenly seemed to just pop out, like dough overflowing in a pan. They exchanged warm smiles and we drove on.

Andrea, of course, was last, but hardly least, in my father's book. She was first and foremost in his mind; a vision of her was a kind of gauze through which everything else flowed. It was true what he said that time: Andrea didn't look fourteen. She could have been twenty, I guess, if you didn't look too close or deep into her eyes. If you just looked at the outline, though—the hair, the chest, the butt, the legs—she looked old enough. Her legs seemed as long as my whole body, and not skinny, either—they had a real, full shape. The three of them in the backseat together certainly filled it up; whereas my little straw body in the front seat by my father only accentuated the empty space I seemed to surround myself with. I was next to invisible.

"Andrea!" my father bellowed as she climbed in. "Welcome."

"Hi, Mr. Lockhart," she said. She was quiet for a girl her size. You just expected more out of her, is what I mean. "Thanks for the ride."

"No problemo," he said.

"Mucho gracias," she replied, ha ha ha, and off we went.

Oh, how I wish I could have thrown myself through the window! I absolutely hated them all—my father, my friends, all of them. As the girls chatted prettily with him, a noise in my ears grew and grew—a white noise, like static. I blocked them out. I sailed away. Any lunatic in the world can stare straight away bug-eyed out the windshield, and that's what I did, creeping down into myself for a better comfort. But occasionally I picked up a transmission.

And how many thousands of boyfriends do you girls have between you? he asked them.

Boys! said Andrea.

They suck! Jennifer said.

Ha ha ha ha ha ha!

Lost in my own space, I watched trees and telephone poles zip by, fences, mailboxes, flowerbeds. Up close the world was a pleasant blur.

Some time went by. I slipped out of my zone, and tuned in to the chatter.

"I'm not sure these are the best directions, Jennifer," my father said, slowing for a light. He stared at the piece of paper Jennifer had given him, frowning. Shook his head. He was on the edge. This is the sort of daddy I was used to.

"Are we lost?" she said.

"I hadn't wanted to use the word," he said, "but I think so, yes."

A chorus of groans, sighs.

"Robin's going to kill us," Andrea said. Already it was the end of the world. You could hear it in her voice.

"How far——."

"I—I have no idea where we are," he said, semi–stuttering. "These directions—I don't know. Some rights are supposed to be lefts, some lefts rights. I mean, I've lived here all my life and I've never even been in this part of town before."

Looking around us, we too realized how far we were from our destination, and what a strange piece of the world we had ended up in. We were at an intersection, and there was a gas station there and a supermarket and a video rental, but they were different than the stores we were used to, with different names on the front and different looking people coming in and out of them. The light turned green and a car behind us honked: they knew we weren't from there. My father pulled into a gas station as if to escape.

"I'm asking for directions," he said, working at keeping that lilt in his voice, but he was straining. He breathed in, then out. "Be right back."

I watched him walk up to the guy there, hands in his trousers, trying to be cool. But he couldn't pull it off: there was something insulated about him, unfamiliar and uncomfortable with the ways of the world. He was not used to getting dirty, talking to gas station attendants and such.

He was a dork, a grown-up, professional dork.

The girls in the back registered as much.

"I can't believe he got us lost," Jennifer said. "Those directions were perfect."

"Shit for brains," Andrea said, laughing, and the car laughed with her—my chuckles preeminent.

"I don't know. The directions probably sucked," Ellen said through her laughter. "Remember the time you got us lost getting to Tim's house?"

"That was not my fault!" she said.

"Whatever."

We were awed by the extent of our removal from our native terrain.

"Where in God's asshole are we?" Andrea said. "I mean, look at this place."

"This is like, another country."

"Somebody help us!" we cried, happier seeming now—

speaking for myself, anyway—than we had been the whole trip.

By the time my father got back the laughter had subsided, and he had revived.

"We're actually not too far out of our way," he said, smiling at the bevy in back. "The skating rink's just a few blocks down this street here."

"Good work, Mr. Lockhart," Andrea said.

"Bravo," said Ellen. "You're our hero."

As we drove the last few blocks, buoyed as I was by that bout of honest, derisive laughter, I wondered if the skating rink would be a fiasco after all. I could overlook the grime, I supposed; and there were some cute boys there, sometimes. I was a pretty good skater too; actually, I could fly as fast as anybody. So I was trying hard to look on the bright side of things when we pulled into the parking lot.

I shouldn't have bothered. It was a dump, a converted barn with a neon sign—RICK'S RINK—tacked on the side. White paint peeled off in scaly sheets. There was a car in the parking lot sitting on big blocks of cement, no wheels at all. It was almost scary. It made you wonder what kind of person Rick was.

"This is definitely not it," Andrea said, sort of painfully.

"It's gotta be," my father said. "There's not another rink around."

"I can't believe Robin would have her party here," Ellen

said. "Look at this place."

"Hey. It's probably a wonderland inside," my father said. "Let's give it a chance. Right, Pumpkin?"

That's when I wanted him to die. To gasp for air, turn blue, then purple, grasp his neck with his hands and slump forward onto the steering wheel. Pumpkin, he said. By such seemingly small and thoughtless disclosures a future is suddenly darkened. I heard Pumpkin on the lips of my friends, playfully at first but occasionally with a mind to hurt; I heard Pumpkin muttered softly, and then like some unrestrained virus making its way through school, Pumpkin, to the girls who were not my friends, and to the boys, until I was finally and utterly Pumpkin, forever and ever.

Thank you, Daddy.

He looked at me. "Did I say something?" he said.

But by then we were out of the car, hovering around the doors, unsure of the wisdom of moving much farther afield before we banded together as a group. My father made a point to lock the car, and then we followed him, like ducks, through the pot-hole filled parking lot to the door of Rick's Rink, which had a picture of a clown painted on the front. But even the clown looked somehow scandalous and leering to me, as if beneath the thin veneer of chalky white face paint was an unshaven and greasy-fingered molester of girls.

"See?" my father said once we got inside. "Nothing to be afraid of. It's just a good old-fashioned family-style rink."

And he was right. Maybe it was a bit scuzzier than some

others, but otherwise not much was amiss. There was the snack bar with the sad-looking woman serving behind it, there were the brightly colored chairs and tables, the video games, and the rink itself, thick with boys and girls, moms and dads, circling, spinning, falling on their asses. There really didn't appear to be much more room out there. Andrea's breasts would take up a whole lane on their own, I thought, and Ellen's thighs—make way!

Robin wasn't there, of course. I knew, as I think the rest of us knew, that we had come to the wrong rink, and that Robin and the rest of her friends were somewhere else, probably not waiting for us anymore because, you know, the party must go on. Meanwhile, we were still lost—only we had decided to pretend not to be. Dad did most of the pretending for us. He told us if Robin had the same directions he did she was probably lost now too, and that she'd be here soon. So he led us up to the stand where we gave them our shoes and rented our skates, and we sat together, lacing up. He hung back, leaned against a pole, and watched us. That was his job, of course, and he was feeling mighty lucky that it was, too. Keep an eye on those girls. Never let your eyes off those girls. He didn't. Jennifer looked up and he smiled. He was happy, but I don't think he included me in the feeling: I existed just beyond the edge of his gaze. There was a sheet of reflective metal along the base of the wall beside me, and as I leaned over lacing up I saw myself, all wavy and distorted, larger than I was in real life, billowing, grotesque— a slight improvement, I thought, over the real thing that was me. The real thing that was me disappeared too easily. The thing in the metal, though horrifying, demanded your attention, couldn't be ignored.

I wish I had this as a mirror on the back of my door, I thought.

And so we skated, round and round. But the boredom set in fairly quickly. The boys there were nothing to look at, and the floor was cracked in places, and a sense of something larger was missing. There was no party here; it was just us, a few girls, skating in circles, pretending. I was willing to put up with the feeling until the time came to go, but the rest of them weren't, I could tell. Something needed to happen.

"Doesn't your dad skate?" Andrea asked as she rolled up beside me. "He looks so lonely over there."

I glanced his way—so did Andrea. He smiled and waved. He was sitting with his legs crossed, drinking a coke, just having the time of his life. If only I could have told her what he was thinking, as he watched her and the rest of them parade around in front of him. But I couldn't give words to it, even though I knew.

"He doesn't skate," I said. "He doesn't do much physical activity like that."

"You call this physical?" She laughed. "It'd be a blast to see him give it a try."

"I really doubt he'd be up to it," I said.

But that wasn't the answer she'd been looking for. She skated away, moving gracefully past a mother and her crying child, until she caught up with Ellen and Jennifer. They conferred briefly, and in a spontaneous giggling girlish rush sped from the rink to his table. Andrea and Jennifer each grabbed an arm while Ellen tugged at his shoes, finally pulling them off to expose his damp, blue-socked feet. He pretended to object, gazing wide-eyed at the perpetrators, gently trying to free himself from their weak grasps, but he was smiling (and blushing!) throughout the entire procedure. By the time Ellen got back with the skates they had released him, but he had submitted to their wishes by then, lacing up without any further prompting, though they stood above him, arms crossed, smiling wickedly.

"I'm going to need some help here," I heard him say as he stood, flailing with his arms like a flightless bird. Jennifer and Ellen were there for him, thank goodness, and they led him from his chair to the metal bar that circled the rink. He gripped it, unsure of any footing at all.

"I'm not sure this is such a good idea," he said. He glanced at me and shrugged his shoulders, rolled his eyes, like *Can you believe these crazy gals?*

"Where's your sense of adventure, Mr. Lockhart?" Andrea asked him.

"I think I left it at home."

"It's fun," Ellen said. "Give it a try."

"We'll help," said Jennifer, as she and Andrea each took an arm. "We're old hands at skating, Mr. Lockhart. Nothing to worry about. As soon as you get the technique down you'll be fine."

But my father was hopeless. Without Andrea and Ellen holding his arms he wouldn't have moved two feet. As it was he appeared to be in a continuous act of falling, saved time and again by the practiced hands of my lovely friends. His own hands brushed against their hips; falling, or almost falling, he clutched their shoulders, their sides. I skated past two or three times, and each time he was touching a different part.

My poor dad.

I circled by them a couple of times, then the next time slowed down.

"Looks like he's about ready," I told them.

They had gone around the rink once already. He appeared to still be grappling with the most basic of mechanics; nothing was working the way it was supposed to. I backpedaled a few feet in front of them, moving with an ease meant to mock. I held my hands out to him.

"Come on, Daddy," I said. "You can do it!"

"I think he needs another lap around," Andrea said.

"With his helpers!" Ellen said, and they laughed, steadying the clumsy monster as best they could.

"Well, he looks ready to me," I said, arms still open wide for him. "What do you think, Dad?"

"I don't know," he said. "I am feeling a bit unsteady."

"You know what you always say," I said. "We don't know what we can do until we try."

And that did it: the decision was made. He straightened up; the girls released their grip. They guided him for a moment, but as soon as he moved toward my hands they let him go, disappearing into the river-world of skaters all around us. Almost miraculously, he stayed erect. Tall and proud, he was skating! I was only a few feet away from him, and was there to catch him if he fell. But as he moved closer to me I glided farther away, and so the distance between us was constant. He lumbered comically onward for a few seconds, somehow managing to stay upright, as though with equal parts of uncertainty in his arms and legs and mind he was able to achieve a kind of quirky balance.

But the most uncertain thing about him was his eyes: they were open, and scared, like a child's eyes. I'd never seen him scared before. I'd never thought of him as being scared, or imagined that he ever was. But here, in this strange building with indoor ice, he didn't know where he was going, or if he could stay up long enough to get there. I knew the feeling. He was alone now with only me to help him, and his thoughts and feelings shone plainly through his eyes.

Can I trust you? His own daughter. He couldn't trust his own daughter. And he knew why, too. He knew why.

I stopped skating, and let the distance close between us. But as his hands approached mine I let our fingertips just touch— and I pulled them back. I thought he'd go right down, face first to the floor, but he didn't. He kept coming at me, moving by one impossible lurch after another, thrashing the air with his arms, finally catching up and bringing me to him in a kind of bear hug, clutching me pressed hard against his chest—and we both went down, together.

"Pumpkin!" he softly whispered as we fell. Pumpkin he called me, like when I was his girl.

CONTRIBUTORS

Rachel Haley Himmelheber's novelette "Happiness Reminders" was published in *McSweeney's*. She is on the editorial staff of Noemi Press.

Shena McAuliffe's fiction has appeared in *Conjunctions* and *Cutbank*. She is the winner of the *Poets and Writers* Missouri Writers Exchange Contest.

Kevin Moffet's collection of stories, *Permanent Visitors*, won the Iowa Short Fiction Prize. His fiction has been published in *Best American Short Stories 2006*, *McSweeney's*, *Tin House*, and elsewhere.

Nicholas Montemarano is the author of a novel, *A Fine Place*, and a collection of short stories, *If The Sky Falls*. He teaches at Franklin & Marshall College.

Christine Schutt is the author of the novel *Florida*, a 2004 National Book Award Finalist, and two story collections.

Daniel Wallace is the author of four novels. The most recent is *Mr. Sebastian and the Negro Magician*. His novel *Big Fish* was made into a film directed by Tim Burton.

Kevin Wilson's stories have appeared in *Ploughshares, New Stories from the South 2005, One Story,* and elsewhere. He serves as the creative writing administrator for the Sewanee Writers Conference.

About the Artist

Steve Keene has shown his work at the Moore College of Art in Philadelphia, Rice University in Houston, the Museum Ludwig in Cologne, Germany, the Santa Monica Museum of Art in Los Angeles, the Linden Centre for Contemporary Art in Melbourne, Australia, the Gulf Coast Museum in Florida, and the Czech Centre in London. Much of his work is inspired by contemporary music and musicians. In recent years, Steve has collaborated with bands including Silver Jews, Pavement, The Apples in Stereo, Soul Coughing, Dave Matthews Band and Merzbow to create album art, video sets, stage sets and posters. Currently he's sold more than 140,000 paintings.

Steve lives and paints in Williamsburg, Brooklyn.